Second Edition

Impact Listening

Jill Robbins
Andrew MacNeill

Series Editor
Michael Rost

2

Published by
Longman Asia ELT
20/F Cornwall House
Taikoo Place
979 King's Road
Quarry Bay
Hong Kong

fax: +852 2856 9578
email: pearsonlongman@pearsoned.com.hk
www.longman.com

and Associated Companies throughout the world.

The publisher's policy is to use **paper manufactured from sustainable forests**

This book was developed for Longman Asia ELT by Lateral Communications Limited.

First edition 2001
This edition 2007
Reprinted 2007

Produced by Pearson Education Asia Limited, Hong Kong
SWTC/02

PROJECT DIRECTOR, SERIES EDITOR: Michael Rost
PROJECT COORDINATOR: Keiko Kimura
PROJECT EDITOR: Aaron Zachmeier
ART DIRECTOR: Inka Mulia
TEXTBOOK DESIGN: Inka Mulia
PRODUCTION COORDINATOR: Rachel Wilson
ILLUSTRATIONS: Ben Shanon, Violet Lemay
PHOTOGRAPHS: Bananastock, Blue Moon, Brand X Pictures, Dynamic Graphics, Iconotect, i dream stock, Image Source, Image Zoo, Inmagine, MIXA, Photodisc, Pixtal, Rubberball, Stockbyte, Tong Ro Image Photographers

AUDIO ENGINEER: Glenn Davidson
MUSIC: Music Bakery
TEST CONSULTANTS: Gary Buck, Natalie Chen
WEBSITE COORDINATOR: Keiko Kimura

IMPACT LISTENING 1
SB + CD ISBN-13: 978-962-00-5801-1 ISBN-10: 962-00-5801-1
TM + Test CDs ISBN-13: 978-962-00-5804-2 ISBN-10: 962-00-5804-6
Class CDs ISBN-13: 978-962-00-5807-3 ISBN-10: 962-00-5807-0

IMPACT LISTENING 2
SB + CD ISBN-13: 978-962-00-5802-8 ISBN-10: 962-00-5802-X
TM + Test CDs ISBN-13: 978-962-00-5805-9 ISBN-10: 962-00-5805-4
Class CDs ISBN-13: 978-962-00-5808-0 ISBN-10: 962-00-5808-9

IMPACT LISTENING 3
SB + CD ISBN-13: 978-962-00-5803-5 ISBN-10: 962-00-5803-8
TM + Test CDs ISBN-13: 978-962-00-5806-6 ISBN-10: 962-00-5806-2
Class CDs ISBN-13: 978-962-00-5809-7 ISBN-10: 962-00-5809-7

Acknowledgements

The authors and editors would like to thank the many teachers and students who have used the Impact Listening series for their feedback. We also wish to thank the following people who contributed ideas, resources, stories, reviews and other feedback that helped us in the development of the second edition of the Impact Listening series:

Glenn Agius
Sara Barrack
Eric Black
Rob Brezny
Richard Carter
Yen-yen Chen
Terry Cox
Sandy Eriksen
Masayoshi Fukui
Ann Gleason
Marvin Greene
William Hayes
Jessie Huang
Jason Jeffries
An-Ran Kim
Barbara Kucer
Ruth Larimer
Jason Lewis
Amy McCormick
Andre Nagel
Tim Odne
John Park
Jessica Raaum
Amy Rubinate
Jerome Schwab
Sherry Shinn
Craig Sweet
Nicke Toree
Joanna Vaughn
J. J. White
Carolyn Wu
Selana Allen
E. Biddlecombe
Erin Boorse
Jennie Brick
Andrea Carvalho
Feodor Chin
Kevin Davey
Christine Feng
Greg Gamaza
Greg Gomina
Scott Grinthal
Patrick Heller
Sarah Hunt
Wonchol Jung
Ju Sook Kim
Norm Lambert
Tae Lee
Li-chun Lu
Alexander Murphy
Dalia Nassar
Jamie Olsen
Jeremy Parsons
Stacey Reeve
Alicia Rydman
Ellen Schwartz
Josh Snyder
Donna Tatsuki
Steven Trost
Yao-yao Wei
Julie Winter
Cesar Zepeda
Kayra Arias
Jennifer Bixby
Christina Boyd
Karen Carrier
Lydia Chen
Jeniffer Cowitz
Payton Davis
Andrew Finch
Mark Girimonte
Allison Gray
Naomi Hagura
James Hobbs
Caroline Hwang
Alex Kahn
Akiko Kimura
Elizabeth Lange
Wayne Lee
Rami Margron
Amy Murphy
Petra Nemcova
Joy Osmanski
Jackie Pels
Kerry Rose
Elly Schottman
Sam Shih
Jim Swan
Steven Thomas
Aurelie Vacheresse
Paul Weisser
Johnny Wong

We also wish to thank our colleagues at Pearson Longman for their guidance and support during the development of the second edition of the series. In particular, we'd like to acknowledge (Hong Kong) Roy Gilbert, Christienne Blodget, Rachel Wilson, Tom Sweeney, Michael Chan, Eric Vogt, Vessela Gasper; (Japan) Shinsuke Ohno, Minoru Ikari, Jonah Glick, Takashi Hata, Yuji Toshinaga, Steve King, Masaharu Nakata, Donn Ogawa, Yuko Tomimasu, Mari Hirukawa, Hiroko Nagashima, Megumi Takemura, Alastair Lamond, Michiyo Mitamura, Ken Sasaki, Takeshi Kamimura, Meiko Naruse, Tomoko Ayuse, Kenji Sakai, Reiko Murota, Mayumi Abe, Minako Uta, Masako Yanagawa, Ayako Tomekawa, Katherine Mackay, Keiko Sugiyama; (Korea) Yong Jin Oh, Chong Dae Chung, Jan Totty, Rilla Roessel, Katherine Ji, Hyuk Jin Kwon, Tae Youp Kim, Sang Ho Bae, Moon Jeong Lim; (Taiwan) Golden Hong, Louis Lin, Constance Mo, Vivian Wang, Sherrie Lin, Christine Huang, Joseph Chan, David Ger; (Thailand) Narerat Ancharepirat, Chris Allen, Unchalee Boonrakvanich, Udom Sathawara, Sura Suksingh;

Special thanks to Jason Lewis, Expedition 360, Maw-Maw's Cajun Kitchen, the rock band Pink, Tech Trek, Maxima Corporation Japan Ltd., Earthfoot Ecotours, Hardscratch Press, $RealMoney$ Enterprises®, Petra Nemcova and Warner Books for permission to use an extract from Love Always, Petra © 2005 Warner Books.

The ***Impact Listening*** series is an innovative set of learning materials that helps students develop listening skills for social, academic and business purposes.

The series has three levels:
Impact Listening 1 (for beginning level students)
Impact Listening 2 (for high-beginning and low-intermediate students)
Impact Listening 3 (for intermediate and high-intermediate students)

Impact Listening makes listening an active and enjoyable experience for students. While featuring an abundance of natural listening input and a variety of creative activities, ***Impact Listening*** leads students to become successful listeners through an effective **4-step process**:

Step 1: Build word-based listening skills

Warm Up

To be successful listeners, we have to hear words and phrases accurately. With the **Warm Up**, each unit begins by helping students understand high-frequency words and phrases. As students become confident in their ability to "catch" common words and phrases, they increase their capacity for listening to longer stretches of language.

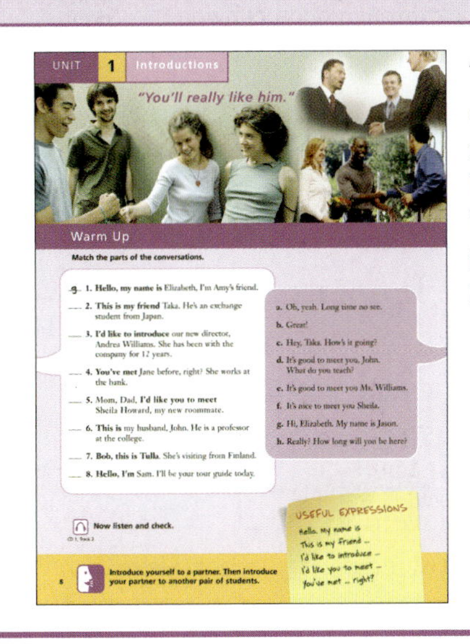
UNIT 1 Introductions

"You'll really like him."

Warm Up

Match the parts of the conversations.

g 1. **Hello, my name is** Elizabeth, I'm Amy's friend.
___ 2. **This is my friend** Taka. He's an exchange student from Japan.
___ 3. **I'd like to introduce** our new director, Andrea Williams. She has been with the company for 12 years.
___ 4. **You've met** Jane before, right? She works at the bank.
___ 5. Mom, Dad, **I'd like you to meet** Sheila Howard, my new roommate.
___ 6. **This is** my husband, John. He is a professor at the college.
___ 7. **Bob, this is Tulla.** She's visiting from Finland.
___ 8. **Hello, I'm** Sam. I'll be your tour guide today.

a. Oh, yeah. Long time no see.
b. Great!
c. Hey, Taka. How's it going?
d. It's good to meet you, John. What do you teach?
e. It's good to meet you Ms. Williams.
f. It's nice to meet you Sheila.
g. Hi, Elizabeth. My name is Jason.
h. Really? How long will you be here?

Now listen and check.

USEFUL EXPRESSIONS
Hello, my name is
This is my friend ...
I'd like to introduce ...
I'd like you to meet ...
You've met ... right?

Introduce yourself to a partner. Then introduce your partner to another pair of students.

8

This section introduces common words and phrases related to the unit theme. With its interactive format, **Warm Up** gets all students involved at the outset of the lesson.

Step 2: Develop focusing strategies

Listening Task

It is important to have a purpose when we listen. Setting a purpose allows the students to become active listeners. In **Listening Task**, students are given a variety of tasks to focus their attention. A short follow-up speaking activity allows students to express their own ideas. They develop active listening strategies: **Prepare**, **Guess**, and **Focus**.

Listening Task

Look at the pictures. Where are the people?

First Listening: Which introductions do the speakers use? Check (✔) the introductions.

1. ✔ "This is ..." ☐ "Hello, I'm ..."
2. ☐ "I'd like you to meet ..." ☐ "I'd like to introduce ..."
3. ☐ "Meet my good friend ..." ☐ "Have you met ..."
4. ☐ "Hi! My name is ..." ☐ "Hi, I'm ..."

Second Listening: How does the other person respond? Check (✔) the response.

1. ✔ "It's good to meet you." ☐ "It's great to meet you."
2. ☐ "Nice to meet you." ☐ "Nice meeting you."
3. ☐ "I think we've met." ☐ "Oh, yeah, we've met."
4. ☐ "Hey." ☐ "Hi."

Act out one of the conversations. Practice with two partners.

9

The section is a set of **two linked tasks** based on short natural listening extracts. The **First Listening** task focuses on understanding the gist, while the **Second Listening** task focuses on details. Vivid illustrations and photographs help students focus on meaning.

Step 3: Practice idea-based strategies

Real World Listening

Everyone experiences difficulties when listening to a second language. While they work on building effective word-based (bottom-up) listening skills, it is also important that students practice idea-based (top-down) listening strategies. In **Real World Listening**, students work on key listening strategies: **Ask**, **Respond**, and **Review**.

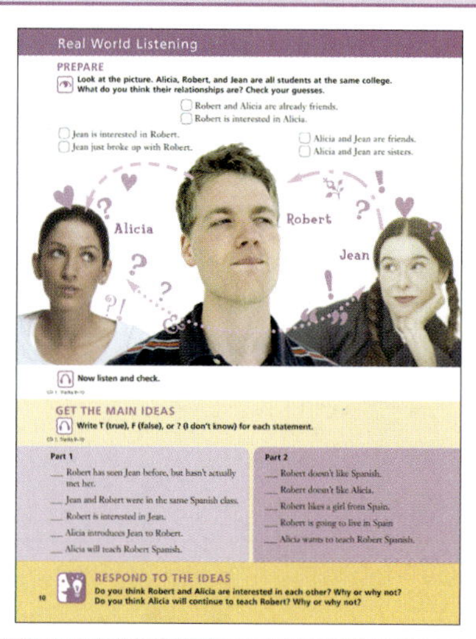
Real World Listening

PREPARE

Look at the picture. Alicia, Robert, and Jean are all students at the same college. What do you think their relationships are? Check your guesses.

- Robert and Alicia are already friends.
- Robert is interested in Alicia.
- Jean is interested in Robert.
- Jean just broke up with Robert.
- Alicia and Jean are friends.
- Alicia and Jean are sisters.

Now listen and check.

GET THE MAIN IDEAS

Write T (true), F (false), or ? (I don't know) for each statement.

Part 1

___ Robert has seen Jean before, but hasn't actually met her.
___ Jean and Robert were in the same Spanish class.
___ Robert is interested in Jean.
___ Alicia introduces Jean to Robert.
___ Alicia will teach Robert Spanish.

Part 2

___ Robert doesn't like Spanish.
___ Robert doesn't like Alicia.
___ Robert likes a girl from Spain.
___ Robert is going to live in Spain
___ Alicia wants to teach Robert Spanish.

RESPOND TO THE IDEAS

Do you think Robert and Alicia are interested in each other? Why or why not?
Do you think Alicia will continue to teach Robert? Why or why not?

10

Based on natural, extended conversations, monologues, and stories, this section helps students develop active listening strategies: predicting, inferring, clarifying, making judgments and responding to the ideas in the extract.

Step 4: Integrate what you have learned

Interaction Link

Connecting to the topic is a vital part of becoming a better listener. Throughout each unit, students are given the opportunity to develop curiosity, activate their knowledge, and express their ideas and opinions. **Interaction Link** helps students link listening and speaking.

Interaction Link

MEET THE CLASS

Get to know your classmates!
Write information about yourself in the chart below.
Then walk around your class and introduce yourself to your classmates.
Ask questions. Find three people you have something in common with.
Write their names in the chart.

TOPIC	Information about me	Classmate with the same answer
My favorite food		
My favorite movie		
Month I was born in		
Something I don't like		
My dream vacation		
My dream job		
My favorite color		
My favorite book		
My favorite song		

Model Conversation 1:

A: Hi, I'm Hideo.
B: Good to meet you. My name's Andrea
A: What's your favorite food?
B: It's spaghetti. What's yours?

Model Conversation 2:

A: Hi, Mario. Have you met Hideo? Hideo, this is Mario
B: Hi, Hideo. Hey, what month were you born in?
C: July. How about you, Mario?
B: September. Why don't you ask Paula? I think she was born in July.

11

Interaction Link is a lively interactive speaking and listening task. Students have the opportunity to review what they have learned in the unit and use interactive tasks to produce real communication.

Impact Listening also includes

Self-Study pages

For use with the Self-Study CD (included in the back of every Student Book), the Self-Study page provides new tasks for the Real World Listening extract, to allow students to review at home. (Answer Key is provided.)

Teacher's Manual

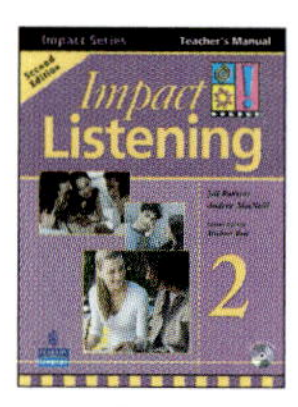

Teachers are encouraged to utilize the *Impact Listening* Teacher's Manual. This manual contains teacher procedures, insightful language and culture notes, full scripts, answer keys, and expansion activities. The Teacher's Manual also includes a Test Master CD-ROM and instructions for creating and administering the tests.

Website

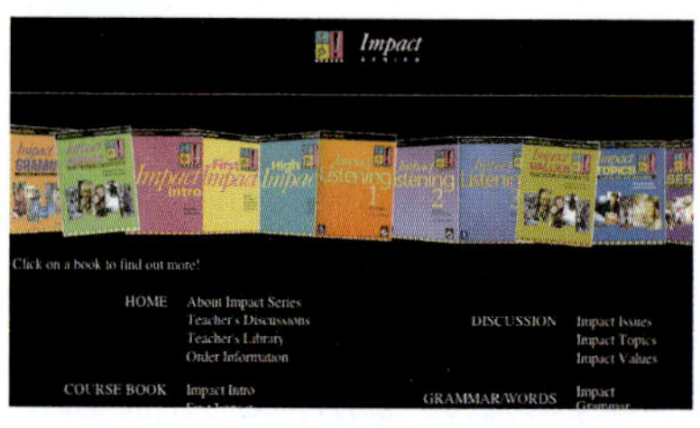

Teachers and students are welcome to use the *Impact Listening* series website for additional ideas and resources.
www.impactseries.com/listening

Impact Listening will help you use listening strategies. Listening strategies are ways of thinking actively as you listen. Here are the main strategies you will practice in this course:

Become an Active Listener

Prepare

- Preparing helps you listen better.
- Before you listen, look at the illustrations and photographs. Think about the ideas.
- Look over the vocabulary words.
- Try to predict what the speakers will say.

Ask

- Good listeners ask a lot of questions.
- While you listen, think of questions: What do you want to know?

Guess

- Guessing can make you a more successful listener.
- Make your best guess at the parts you don't understand.

Respond

- Responding is part of listening!
- While you listen, pay attention to the speaker's ideas and intentions.
- After you listen, respond to the ideas: What do you think?

Focus

- Focus = Listen with a purpose.
- Before you listen, look at the listening task or questions.
- While you listen, focus on the task and questions. Listen for key words.
- If there are some words you don't understand, that's OK. Keep listening.

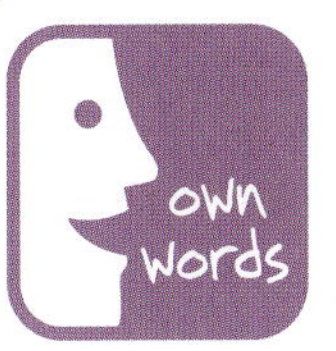

Review

- Reviewing builds your "listening memory."
- After you listen, think about the meaning of what the speakers have said.
- Try to say the meaning in your own words.

"You'll really like him."

Warm Up

 **Match the parts of the conversations.**

g 1. **Hello, my name is** Elizabeth. I'm Amy's friend.

___ 2. **This is my friend** Taka. He's an exchange student from Japan.

___ 3. **I'd like to introduce** our new director, Andrea Williams. She's been with the company for twelve years.

___ 4. **You've met** Jane before, right? She works at the bank.

___ 5. Mom, Dad, **I'd like you to meet** Sheila Howard, my new roommate.

___ 6. **This is** my husband, John. He's a professor at the college.

___ 7. Bob, **this is** Tulla. She's visiting from Finland.

___ 8. **Hello, I'm** Sam. I'll be your tour guide today.

a. Oh, yeah. Long time no see.

b. Great!

c. Hey, Taka. How's it going?

d. It's good to meet you, John. What do you teach?

e. It's good to meet you, Ms. Williams.

f. It's nice to meet you, Sheila.

g. Hi, Elizabeth. My name is Jason.

h. Really? How long will you be here?

Now listen and check.

CD 1, Track 2

USEFUL EXPRESSIONS

Hello. My name is ...
This is my friend ...
I'd like to introduce ...
I'd like you to meet ...
You've met ... right?

 **Introduce yourself to a partner. Then introduce your partner to another pair of students.**

Look at the pictures. Where are the people?

CD 1, Tracks 3–7

First Listening: **Which introductions do the speakers use? Check (✔) the introductions.**

1

☑ "This is ..."

☐ "Hello, I'm ..."

2

☐ "I'd like you to meet ..."

☐ "I'd like to introduce ..."

3

☐ "Meet my good friend ..."

☐ "Have you met ..."

4

☐ "Hi! My name is ..."

☐ "Hi, I'm ..."

CD 1, Tracks 3–7

Second Listening: **How does the other person respond? Check (✔) the response.**

1. 

☑ "It's good to meet you."

☐ "It's great to meet you."

2. ☐ "Nice to meet you."

☐ "Nice meeting you."

3. ☐ "I think we've met."

☐ "Oh, yeah, we've met."

4. 

☐ "Hey."

☐ "Hi."

Act out one of the conversations. Practice with two partners.

Real World Listening

PREPARE

Look at the picture. Jean, Alicia, and Robert are all students at the same college. What do you think their relationships are? Check your guesses.

- ☐ Robert and Alicia are already friends.
- ☐ Robert is interested in Alicia.
- ☐ Jean is interested in Robert.
- ☐ Jean just broke up with Robert.
- ☐ Alicia and Jean are friends.
- ☐ Alicia and Jean are sisters.

Now listen and check.

CD 1, Tracks 8–10

GET THE MAIN IDEAS

Write T (true), F (false), or ? (I don't know) for each statement.

CD 1, Tracks 8–10

Part 1

___ Robert has seen Jean before but hasn't actually met her.

___ Jean and Robert were in the same Spanish class.

___ Robert is interested in Jean.

___ Alicia introduces Jean to Robert.

___ Alicia will teach Robert Spanish.

Part 2

___ Robert doesn't like Spanish.

___ Robert doesn't like Alicia.

___ Robert likes a girl from Spain.

___ Robert is going to live in Spain.

___ Alicia wants to teach Robert Spanish.

RESPOND TO THE IDEAS

Do you think Robert and Alicia are interested in each other? Why or why not?
Do you think Alicia will continue to teach Robert? Why or why not?

MEET THE CLASS

Get to know your classmates!
Write information about yourself in the chart below.
Then walk around your class and introduce yourself to your classmates.
Ask questions. Find three people you have something in common with.
Write their names in the chart.

TOPIC	Information about me	Classmate with the same answer
My favorite food		
My favorite movie		
Month I was born		
Something I don't like		
My dream vacation		
My dream job		
My favorite color		
My favorite book		
My favorite song		

Model Conversation 1

A: Hi, I'm Hideo.
B: Good to meet you. My name's Andrea.
A: What's your favorite food?
B: It's spaghetti. What's yours?

Model Conversation 2

A: Hi, Mario. Have you met Hideo? Hideo, this is Mario.
B: Hi, Hideo. Hey, what month were you born in?
C: July. How about you, Mario?
B: September. Why don't you ask Paula? I think she was born in July.

UNIT 2 Personality

"What do you like about him?"

Warm Up

Write the missing words.

sincere
dependable
honest

Angela

1. I think friends have to be honest. I can't stand it when my friends don't tell the truth. If my friends are __________ I know they're __________, too. I can count on them, you know?

shy
outgoing
friendly

2. I seem to end up with people who are a lot more __________ than I am—the friendly type, you know, talkative and __________. I'm kind of __________ and quiet myself, so I let them do the talking.

David

kind-hearted
easygoing
mature

Amy

3. I like people who are __________, but __________ enough to be responsible for themselves. Life can be so stressful. I need people who are __________ and can help me when I'm in trouble.

critical
assertive
cheerful

4. I have a lot of friends on my soccer team who are pretty __________–even aggressive. But we win a lot, so that makes me happy. I'm usually __________, so I don't like being with people who are too __________—always complaining about things.

Ali

Now listen and check.

CD 1, Track 11

USEFUL EXPRESSIONS

I'm basically a ... person.
I think some people are too ...
... is a really good quality.
I get along best with ... people.
Most of my friends are ...

What kind of people do you like? What kind of people does your partner like?

Listening Task

Look at the pictures. What are the people like?

First Listening: Who are the speakers talking about?

CD 1, Tracks 12–18

1 her dad

2 ____________

3 ____________

4 ____________

5 ____________

6 ____________

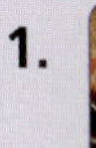

Second Listening: Check the qualities each speaker mentions.

CD 1, Tracks 12–18

1. 
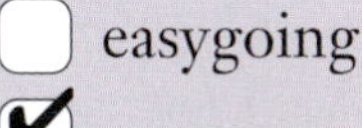
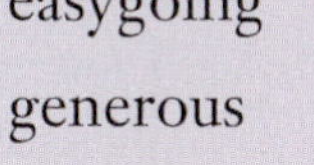
   - [ ] easygoing
   - [x] generous

2. 
   - [ ] silly
   - [ ] moody

3. 
   - [ ] energetic
   - [ ] aggressive

4. - [ ] sincere
   - [ ] weird

5. 
   - [ ] defensive
   - [ ] dependable

6. 
   - [ ] lazy
   - [ ] laid-back

Tell your partner about a friend, a family member, or a teacher.

PREPARE

What kind of person are you? Check your answers.

Do you like to ...

spend time alone?	☐ yes	☐ no	eat at nice restaurants?	☐ yes	☐ no	plan ahead?	☐ yes	☐ no
work in groups?	☐ yes	☐ no	ask questions in class?	☐ yes	☐ no	follow directions?	☐ yes	☐ no

Now listen to Part 1 of the personality quiz and write the missing phrases.

CD 1, Tracks 19–20

GET THE MAIN IDEAS

Listen to Part 1 again. Circle your answers.

CD 1, Track 20

When I ...	I prefer to ...	I'd rather ...
1. watch a movie	**a.** watch alone	**b.** watch with others
2.	**a.** work by myself	**b.** work with a group
3.	**a.** make reservations	**b.** just go
4.	**a.** read the instructions	**b.** connect it without instructions
5.	**a.** tell my ideas first	**b.** listen to others first
6.	**a.** ask myself	**b.** let someone else ask

Now listen to Part 2. Check the characteristic that describes you for each set of questions.

CD 1, Track 21

1 & 2 ☐ independent ☐ dependent
3 & 4 ☐ organized ☐ creative
5 & 6 ☐ leader ☐ follower

RESPOND TO THE IDEAS

Compare answers with a partner. Are you similar or different? Do you agree with the personality quiz? Why or why not?

IT'S A MATCH

1. Answer the questions about yourself.

2. Ask your classmates the same questions. Write the names of classmates who have the same answers.

	Me	Classmate
Do you like to play music?		
Are you shy?		
Do you like to talk about serious things?		
Are you athletic?		
Do you like to talk to people?		
Are you outgoing?		
Do you love to exercise?		
Do you like quiet people?		
Are you sensitive?		
Do you love cats?		
Do you love dogs?		
Do you like technology?		
Do you like to tell stories?		
Do you like challenges?		
Are you quiet?		
Do you like to tell jokes?		

Warm Up

Write the missing words.

apartment
roommate
housing
sharing

1. Rob and Jeannie are talking after class.

Rob: Hey, what are you doing after class?
Jeannie: I'm going over to the housing office.
Rob: Looking for an __________?
Jeannie: No, we need a __________.
Rob: Oh, you're __________ a place?

reasonable
furniture
rent
available
studio

2. Jorge is talking to an agent in a real estate office.

Agent: We have a __________ that's __________. That's one large room, basically.
Jorge: Is it furnished?
Agent: No, you have to bring your own __________.
Jorge: How much is the __________?
Agent: It's very __________.

move out
check
refund
deposit

3. Hoon is paying the deposit at his new apartment.

Hoon: Here's the __________, Mrs. Anderson.
Mrs. Anderson: Thanks. That will cover your __________.
Hoon: Will I get that money back when I __________?
Mrs. Anderson: Yes, if nothing is broken, you'll get a __________.
Hoon: OK, I'll be careful.

Now listen and check.

CD 1, Track 22

USEFUL EXPRESSIONS

What kind of place do you live in?
What do you like about it?
How much is the rent?
Is it in a good neighborhood?
Is it close to ... ?

Find out what kind of place your partner lives in. What does he or she like and dislike about it?

Listening Task

Look at the pictures. Who do the people live with?

First Listening: What are the living situations?

CD 1, Tracks 23–27

1

Tim lives
- ☑ with his parents.
- ☐ with his brother.
- ☐ by himself.

2

David lives
- ☐ in an apartment.
- ☐ in a dorm.
- ☐ in a fraternity house.

3

Reina lives
- ☐ with a roommate.
- ☐ with her cat.
- ☐ in a noisy neighborhood.

4

Nate lives
- ☐ on a friend's couch.
- ☐ alone with his dog.
- ☐ with a lot of roommates.

Second Listening: What does each speaker like or dislike about the situation?

CD 1, Tracks 23–27

1.  Tim likes
   - ☑ family relationships. 
   - ☐ rules.

2.  David likes
   - ☐ privacy.
   - ☐ convenience.

3.  Reina doesn't like
   - ☐ the commuting time. 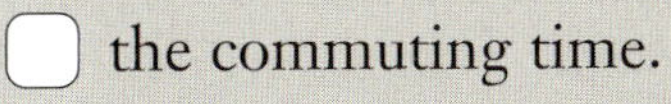
   - ☐ noisy roommates. 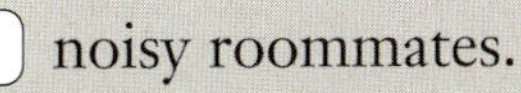

4.  Nate doesn't like
   - ☐ the high cost of rent.
   - ☐ the lack of freedom.

What kind of place would you like to live in? Why?

PREPARE

Hye Jun is visiting two places to live while she's at school. What do you think each place is like? Look at the advertisements and put the words below in the correct categories.

STUDIO APT, lots of room, close to city center, $950, call 555-8736.

clean	fun	convenient	loud
messy	private	crowded	quiet

Apartment	Shared house

Now listen and check.

CD 1, Tracks 28-30

GET THE MAIN IDEAS

What are some good things about each place? Some bad things?

CD 1, Tracks 28-30

	Good things	Bad things
Apartment		
Shared house		

RESPOND TO THE IDEAS

Which place do you think Hye Jun will choose? Why?
What is important to you when you choose a place to live?

MY PLACE

Describe your room to your partner and have him/her draw it as you describe it. Then draw your partner's room based on his/her description. Join with another pair and take turns describing the rooms in the pictures you drew. Use the words in the box.

desk	bed	table	window	plant
couch	chair	carpet	poster	shelf

MY ROOM

MY PARTNER'S ROOM

UNIT 4 Technology

Warm Up

Choose the correct words and phrases.

1. MP3 players make it possible to ☑ **hook up to** ☐ **check out** your computer and ☐ **download** ☐ **subtract** music to listen to.
2. Digital cameras are convenient. They enable you to ☐ **burn** ☐ **upload** photos to your computer and ☐ **send** ☐ **take** them by e-mail.
3. Cell phones let you ☐ **buy** ☐ **snap** photos and ☐ **send** ☐ **click** text messages to your friends.
4. You can ☐ **erase** ☐ **keep track of** appointments and ☐ **store** ☐ **scan** contact information on your PDA.
5. My new computer enables me to ☐ **shut down** ☐ **log on** to my favorite sites. I can also ☐ **detect** ☐ **burn** CDs and DVDs.

Now listen and check.

CD 1, Track 31

USEFUL EXPRESSIONS

It lets you ...
It allows you to ...
It's great because ...
It makes it possible to ...
It's hard to use.

What kinds of technology do you like?
What kinds of technology do you dislike?
Ask your partner.

Listening Task

Look at the pictures. What types of gadgets do you see?

First Listening: What are the speakers doing?

CD 1, Tracks 32–36

1

- [ ] taking a picture
- [x] watching a video
- [ ] downloading music
- [ ] making a phone call

2

- [ ] watching a video
- [ ] e-mailing a friend
- [ ] downloading music
- [ ] listening to the radio

3

- [ ] playing a game
- [ ] adding numbers
- [ ] looking up information
- [ ] sending an e-mail

4

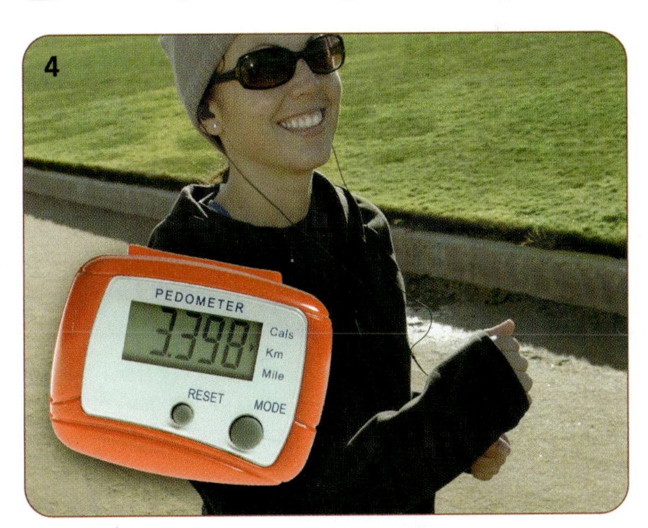

- [ ] checking blood pressure
- [ ] measuring the distance she walks
- [ ] running a race
- [ ] measuring calories

Second Listening: What does the speaker dislike about the technology?

CD 1, Tracks 32–36

1.
- [x] The screen is too small.
- [ ] He can't get text messages.

2.
- [ ] It costs money.
- [ ] There aren't any good songs.

3.
- [ ] It doesn't send e-mail.
- [ ] It's hard to use.

4.
- [ ] It beeps too much.
- [ ] It vibrates too much.

Do you have any of the items that the speakers have? What can they do? Ask your partner about the technology they use.

PREPARE

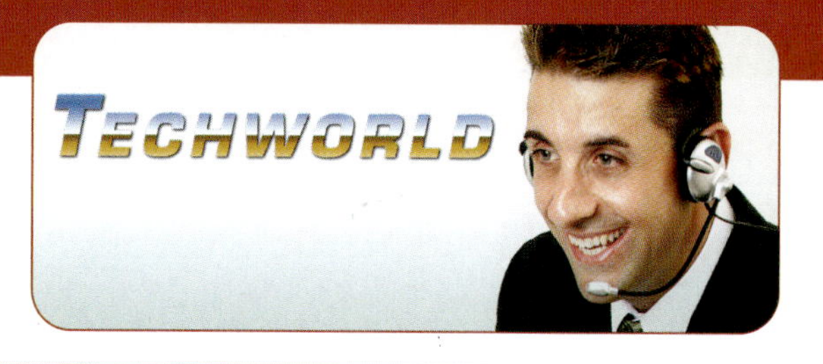

Look at the pictures. Zack Newton, the host of *Techworld*, is interviewing two inventors. What do you think the inventions do?

- ☐ talks to you
- ☐ goes to class for you
- ☐ does homework for you
- ☐ teaches things to you
- ☐ makes friends for you

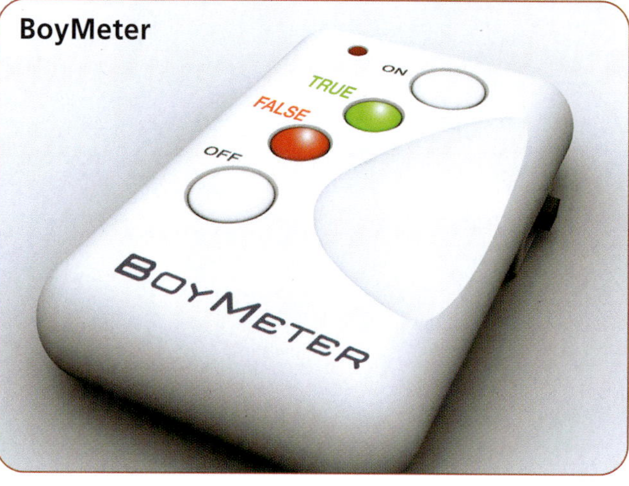

- ☐ locates your boyfriend
- ☐ finds out if someone is telling the truth
- ☐ finds out if someone really likes you
- ☐ finds out someone's age
- ☐ makes a boy like you

Now listen and check.

CD 1, Tracks 37–39 (Track 8)

GET THE MAIN IDEAS

Write T (true), F (false), or ? (I don't know) for each statement.

CD 1, Tracks 37–39

MeBot

- ☐ It gets good grades.
- ☐ It goes to classes.
- ☐ It teaches classes.
- ☐ It cheats.
- ☐ It kills brain cells.
- ☐ It costs too much.
- ☐ It makes students lazy.
- ☐ It makes teachers happy.

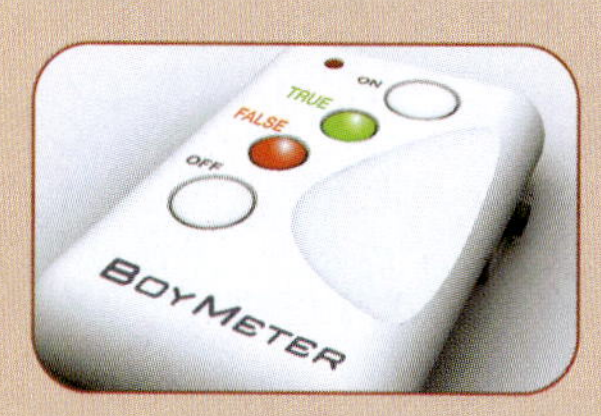

BoyMeter

- ☐ It reads people's minds.
- ☐ It detects the truth.
- ☐ It costs too much.
- ☐ It drinks too much.
- ☐ It makes loud noises.
- ☐ It doesn't always work.
- ☐ It weighs a lot.
- ☐ It only works on boys.

RESPOND TO THE IDEAS

Which of the inventions would you like to have? Why?
What would you like to invent? Why?

WHAT DOES IT DO?

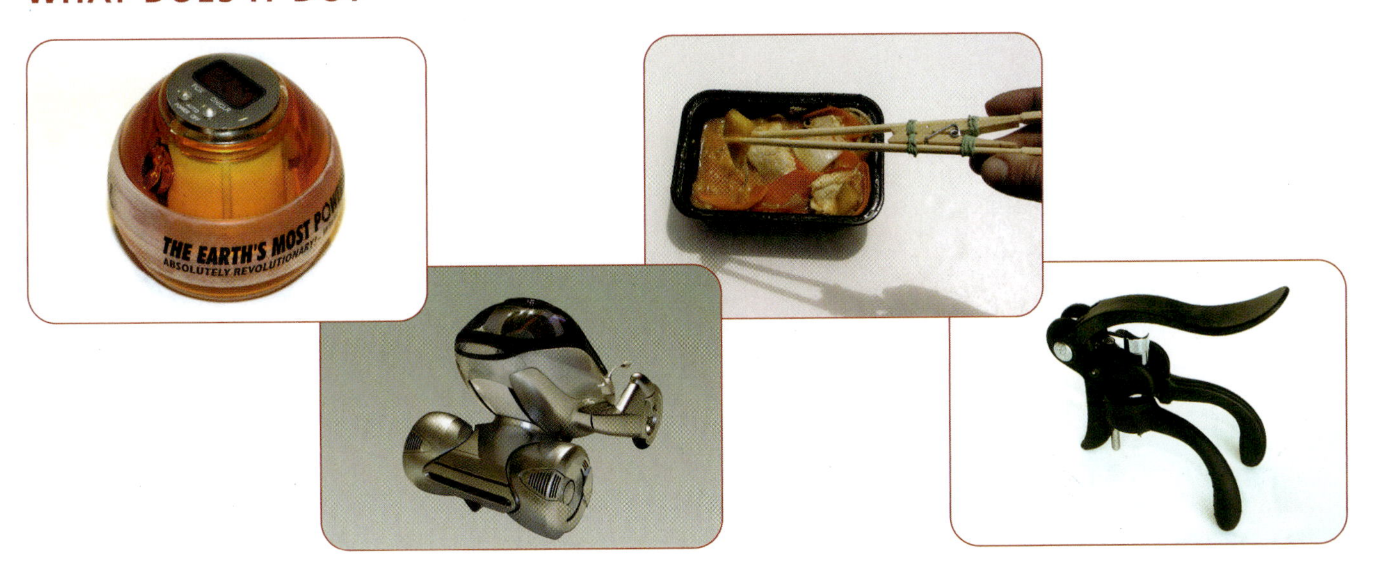

1. Work in groups. Think of a new invention. It can be serious or silly, useful or useless. Give your invention a name, draw it, and write what it does.

What is it called?	What does it look like?	What does it do?

2. Tell the class about your invention. Explain what it does and how it works. Use the phrases in the box.

> It allows you to …
> It enables you to …
> It lets you …
> It makes it possible to …
> It has the ability to …

Warm Up

 **Write the missing words.**

abroad	stared	advice	locals	regret
foreigner	healthy	open	gesture	pointed

1. I was in Spain for about a month. I regret spending so much time with my friends from home. I wish I'd gone out more alone, so I could meet some ________.

2. I went to Korea, and I can't speak any Korean, so I had to ________ to let people know what I wanted. Like, I ________ at pictures of food on the menu to order in a restaurant. I wish I'd learned the language a little.

3. I went to the U.S. by myself. If you're going to travel ________, my ________ is to go with a friend. Sometimes I really got scared because I was alone. I should have gone with someone else.

4. I traveled in Mongolia, and I really felt like a ________. People ________ at me when I walked down the street. But I think people were just curious. I did look different.

5. I was in New Zealand. It was really cool. Everyone was so friendly there, so ________. And there was nature everywhere. I felt so ________ when I was there.

 **Now listen and check.**

CD 1, Track 40

USEFUL EXPRESSIONS

Tell me about ...
Have you ever been to ... ?
Do you speak ... ?
What do you think of ... ?
What did you like about it?

 **Have you visited a foreign country? Are you interested in studying in a foreign country? Ask a partner.**

Listening Task

Look at the pictures. Where are the people?

First Listening:

Where did each student travel?

CD 1, Tracks 41–44

1. China
2.
3.

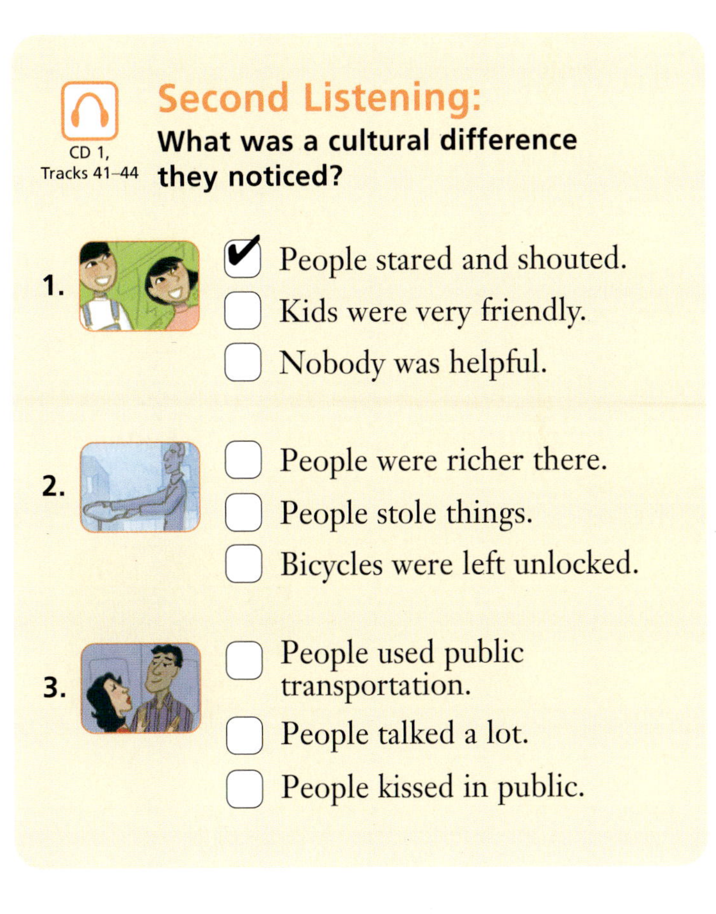

Second Listening:

What was a cultural difference they noticed?

CD 1, Tracks 41–44

1.
- [x] People stared and shouted.
- [ ] Kids were very friendly.
- [ ] Nobody was helpful.

2.
- [ ] People were richer there.
- [ ] People stole things.
- [ ] Bicycles were left unlocked.

3.
- [ ] People used public transportation.
- [ ] People talked a lot.
- [ ] People kissed in public.

Which of these places sounds interesting to you? Are the cultures the same as yours or different? Ask your partner.

PREPARE

Look at the pictures. Leath and Hannah are talking about Zambia. What do you think they will mention? (Choose two.)

- ☐ natural beauty
- ☐ political problems
- ☐ poverty
- ☐ natural resources
- ☐ animals
- ☐ schools
- ☐ families
- ☐ clothes

Now listen and check.

CD 1, Tracks 45–47

GET THE MAIN IDEAS

Here are some opinions about Zambia. Write L if Leath would agree, H if Hannah would agree, and L+H if both would agree.

CD 1, Tracks 45–47

Leath

Hannah

___ I love the people in Zambia.

___ Living in Zambia was a powerful experience.

___ Zambia has a lot of poverty.

___ Zambia faces a lot of problems.

___ I would love to go back to Zambia.

___ Zambia is a healthy place to be.

___ Zambia has a lot of natural beauty.

___ I feel sorry for the people who live in Zambia.

RESPOND TO THE IDEAS

What would a visitor think of your country? Why?

TRAVEL SURVEY

1. Form a group. Choose three of the questions below. Walk around the room and get three answers for each question.

2. Return to your group. Make a chart to show how other students answered your group's questions. Present your findings to the class.

Sample questions:

1. Have you ever been to a foreign country? (sample chart below)

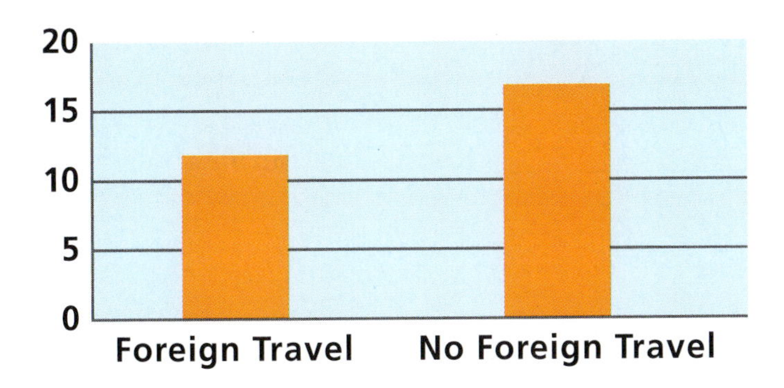

2. Do you like to travel alone or with a friend?

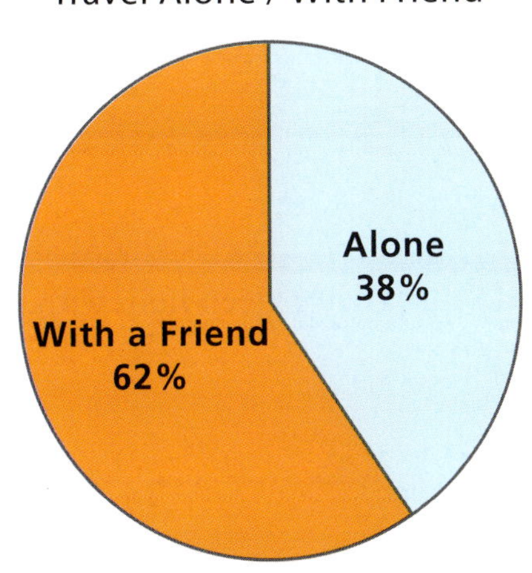

3. If you could go anywhere in the world, where would you go?
4. How many times have you traveled this year?
5. What is the best way to travel? (plane, train, boat, car, bus)
6. Do you prefer budget travel or luxury travel?
7. What is the best season for traveling?

PART 1. Hearing the correct words.

Listen and write the missing words.

CD 1, Track 48

1. I'd ________________________ the new principal, Bertha Rivas. She has been with the school district for twelve years.

2. Honey, I'd ________________________ Rob Unger, our new neighbor.

3. It's ________________________, Mr. Unger.

4. I'm ________________________, so I don't like being with people who are silly—________________________ about things.

5. School can be ________________________, but my classmates are ________________________ and help me when I need help with my homework.

6. I like to hang out with people who are ________________________ I am.

7. This is the ________________________. It's this one large room with a small bathroom.

8. I need an apartment that is ________________________. I don't have ________________________.

9. How much money will I get back when ______________________________?

10. I can ______________________________ to my computer and ______________________________. I watch them while I'm on the train.

11. Oh, great! I finally found my PDA. I really ______________________________. It has my calendar where I ______________________________ of my daily schedule.

12. I can't live without my ______________________________. I've just got to have my music with me wherever I go.

13. You know, you learn ______________________________ about yourself when you travel abroad. You not only learn about ______________________________, you learn more about your own culture, too.

14. Now that Melissa has been to Europe, she's more ______________________________ with foreigners she meets.

15. When you don't speak the language in a new country, you often ______________________________ to let people know what you want.

PART 2. Understanding conversations.

Listen to each conversation. Then circle the answers.

CD 1, Tracks 49–58

1. Where is Alicia from?
   - (a) She is from Spain.
   - (b) She is from Mexico.
   - (c) She is from the United States.

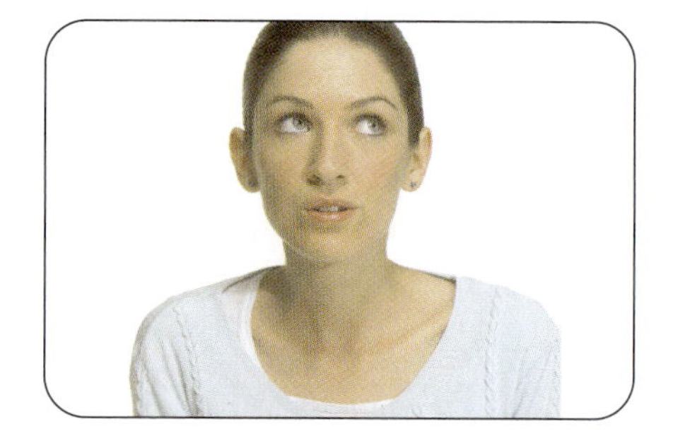

2. Why does Robert want to learn Spanish?
   - (a) His family is from Spain.
   - (b) He will be an exchange student in Spain.
   - (c) He will visit a girl in Spain.

3. How does the speaker describe her boyfriend?
   - (a) He is really down-to-earth.
   - (b) He is sincere.
   - (c) Both **a** and **b**

4. How does the speaker describe himself?
   - (a) Talkative and friendly
   - (b) Shy and quiet
   - (c) Intelligent and talkative

5. When will the speakers go to dinner?
   - (a) At 10:00
   - (b) On Friday
   - (c) Today after class

6. What advice does Reina's friend give her?

(a) To ask her roommate to move out

(b) To look for a new apartment

(c) To move into her apartment

7. What technology are the speakers using?

(a) They are using a television.

(b) They are using a cell phone.

(c) They are using a computer.

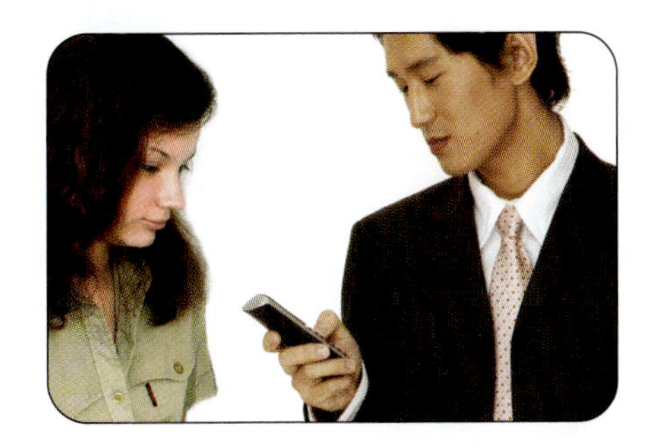

8. Who has a PDA?

(a) Both speakers

(b) The man only

(c) The woman only

9. How did Julia get around in Amsterdam?

(a) She walked.

(b) She stole a bike.

(c) She rented a bike.

10. What does Wendy think about what Jim says?

(a) She doesn't like it.

(b) She thinks it's strange.

(c) She thinks it's nice.

"What's your number?"

Warm Up

Kim has just met Eric at a coffee shop. Which questions are OK for her to ask? Which ones are too private?

1. What's your name?	☑ OK	☐ Private
2. How old are you?	☐ OK	☐ Private
3. Do you have a girlfriend (boyfriend)?	☐ OK	☐ Private
4. Can I have your phone number?	☐ OK	☐ Private
5. Can I have your e-mail address?	☐ OK	☐ Private
6. Where do you live?	☐ OK	☐ Private
7. How much do you weigh?	☐ OK	☐ Private
8. How much money do you make?	☐ OK	☐ Private
9. Do you dye your hair?	☐ OK	☐ Private
10. What do your parents do?	☐ OK	☐ Private
11. Do you have any brothers or sisters?	☐ OK	☐ Private
12. Do you have any children?	☐ OK	☐ Private

Now listen and check.

CD 1, Track 59

USEFUL EXPRESSIONS

That's something I don't share.
I'd rather not say.
I prefer not to give my ...
I don't share that.
I'd like to keep that private.

Ask your partner these questions. Which questions would your partner rather not answer?

Listening Task

Look at the pictures. Where are the people?

First Listening: What information is the speaker asked for?

CD 1, Tracks 60–64

1

- [ ] address
- [ ] telephone number
- [ ] name

2

- [ ] e-mail address
- [ ] home address
- [ ] age

3

- [ ] home address
- [ ] telephone number
- [ ] credit card number

4

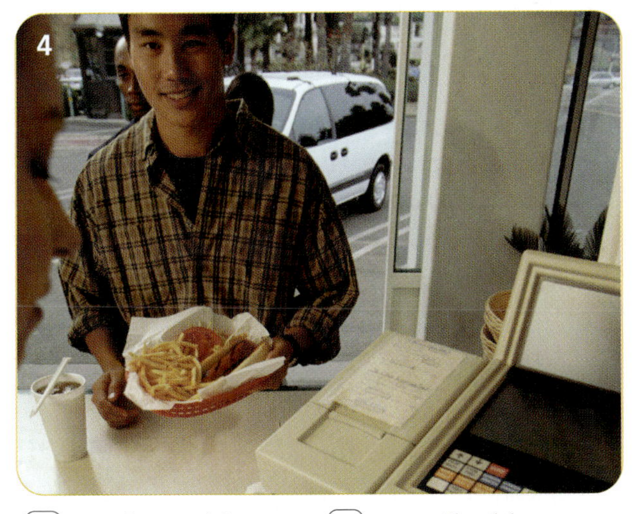

- [ ] mailing address
- [ ] e-mail address
- [ ] zip code

Second Listening: Does the speaker give the information?

CD 1, Tracks 60–64

1. [ ] yes [ ] no [ ] part of it
2. [ ] yes [ ] no [ ] part of it
3. [ ] yes [ ] no [ ] part of it
4. [ ] yes [ ] no [ ] part of it

Act out one of the conversations with your partner.

PREPARE

Catherine is at a party. She's going to meet a guy named Chip. Do you think she will like him? Why or why not?

She'll like him because …	She won't like him because …
☐ he is very handsome.	☐ he isn't very handsome.
☐ he is very polite.	☐ he isn't very polite.
☐ he is very educated.	☐ he isn't very educated.
☐ he dresses very well.	☐ he doesn't dress very well.
☐ he talks very smoothly.	☐ he doesn't talk very smoothly.

Now listen to Part 1 only and check.

CD 1, Tracks 65–66

GET THE MAIN IDEAS

Listen to Part 1 again. How does Catherine answer Chip's questions?

CD 1, Track 66

	Directly	Indirectly	Doesn't answer
It's a cool party, isn't it?	☐	☐	☐
How's it going?	☐	☐	☐
What's your name?	☐	☐	☐
Catherine what?	☐	☐	☐
Are you having a good time?	☐	☐	☐
Do you live around here?	☐	☐	☐
Where do you live?	☐	☐	☐
What's your phone number?	☐	☐	☐
How about your e-mail address?	☐	☐	☐
Do you have a boyfriend?	☐	☐	☐

RESPOND TO THE IDEAS

Listen to Part 2. What does Catherine think of Chip? What do you think of Chip?

CD 1, Track 67

THAT'S KIND OF PERSONAL!

1. **Which questions are appropriate for the following people to ask? Which questions are not appropriate? Write the numbers of the questions in the columns.**

1. What's your name?
2. How old are you?
3. Do you have a boyfriend/girlfriend?
4. Can I have your phone number?
5. Can I have your e-mail address?
6. Where do you live?
7. How much do you weigh?
8. How much money do you make?
9. Do you dye your hair?
10. What do your parents do?
11. Do you have any children?
12. Do you believe in God?

Situation	Appropriate	Not appropriate
Doctor asking a patient		
Boss asking an employee		
Friend asking a friend		
Someone you are attracted to asking you		
Someone you are not attracted to asking you		
Your idea:		

2. **Compare your responses with a classmate's answers. Discuss why you answered the way you did.**

3. **Optional: Compare your answers with other pairs. Report your findings to the class.**

   We found that most students feel that it is OK for a doctor to ask a patient how old they are. We also found that it is not appropriate for a doctor to ask a patient ...

UNIT 7 Family

"I really take after my dad."

Warm Up

Write the words with the same meaning.

brother-in-law	parents	stepmother	son-in-law
niece	adopted	cousins	nephews

1. My **brother's daughter** (__niece__) is so cute. I think she looks like me.
2. I get along pretty well with my **dad's new wife** (________). She's actually pretty nice.
3. When I was little, I used to spend a lot of time with my **uncle's children** (________). They were like my brothers and sisters.
4. Everybody had a great time at my sister's wedding. My **sister's new husband** (________) was even dancing on the tables. What a nut!
5. I'm not in a hurry to have kids yet. I spend a lot of time with my **brother's three boys** (________) and I know they can be a handful.
6. Ted and Jane are really happy to have Lina. They **made** her **their legal child** (________ her) when she was just three months old.
7. Betty's daughter got married yesterday. Her **daughter's husband** (________) is a lawyer.
8. My **mother and father** (________) met when they were in high school. They've been married for twenty-five years.

Now listen and check.

CD 1, Track 68

USEFUL EXPRESSIONS

Are you two related?
How are you related to ... ?
I look like my ...
I take after my ...
We get along really well.

Tell your partner about two people in your family.

Listening Task

Look at the picture. How are the people related?

First Listening: Sara is looking at a family photo with a friend. Who is she talking about?

CD 1, Tracks 69–75

1. ______ 2. ______ 3. ______

4. ______ 5. ______ 6. ______

Second Listening: How does she describe each relative?

CD 1, Tracks 69–75

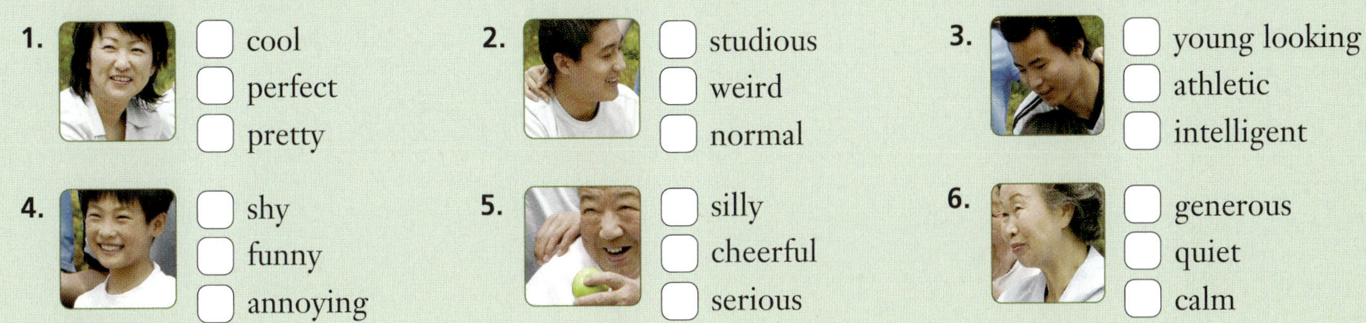

1. ☐ cool ☐ perfect ☐ pretty
2. ☐ studious ☐ weird ☐ normal
3. ☐ young looking ☐ athletic ☐ intelligent
4. ☐ shy ☐ funny ☐ annoying
5. ☐ silly ☐ cheerful ☐ serious
6. ☐ generous ☐ quiet ☐ calm

Who do you get along with best in your family? Why?

PREPARE

Look at these pictures of Jane and her parents. Which parent does Jane look like most? Which parent do you think she takes after?

Looks like	Takes after
☐ Mom ☐ Dad	☐ Mom ☐ Dad

Now listen and check.

CD 1, Tracks 76–77

GET THE MAIN IDEAS

What does Jane have in common with her mom? What about her dad? Write two things for each parent.

CD 1, Tracks 76–77

Mom	Dad

RESPOND TO THE IDEAS

Do you think Jane is more like her mother or father? Why?
Which of your parents are you most like? Discuss your answers with a partner.

SOMETHING IN COMMON

1. Write the names of five family members and how they're related to you (sister, brother, uncle, mother) in the chart. Then write something that you have in common for each of the categories.

2. Ask a partner about what he or she has in common with his or her family members.

Family member	What do you have in common?
1.	Appearance
	Personality
	Interests
2.	Appearance
	Personality
	Interests
3.	Appearance
	Personality
	Interests
4.	Appearance
	Personality
	Interests
5.	Appearance
	Personality
	Interests

Warm Up

Write the missing words and phrases.

get off	blocks	take	corner
get on	get	go down	catch

1. Washington Park? Let's see. Take the number 8 bus and get off on Jefferson Street.
2. The library? Um, you can walk there from here. It's only three ___________.
3. The stadium is kind of far. ___________ the freeway and take the Seventh Avenue exit.
4. The post office? That's easy. Just ___________ that street over there. It'll be on your left.
5. The university? Mm, I think the best way is to ___________ the subway. It's on the Green Line.
6. I think you have to take a taxi to get to the airport. You can ___________ one in front of your hotel.
7. The zoo? Ah. I think there's a train that goes there. You can ___________ it at Central Station.
8. Oh, the supermarket? It's right around the ___________.

Now listen and check.

CD 1, Track 78

USEFUL EXPRESSIONS

Can you tell me where ... is?
How do you get to ...?
Do you know where ... is?
You'll see a ... on the ...
Your best bet is to ...

Ask a partner how to get to a well-known place in your city.

Look at the photos. Do you know where they were taken?

First Listening: What are they looking for?

CD 1, Tracks 79–85

1

2

3

4

5

6

Second Listening: How do they ask for directions?

CD 1, Tracks 79–85

1. ☐ I'm looking for …
   ☐ Do you know where … ?
2. ☐ Where is … ?
   ☐ Do you know where … ?
3. ☐ Tell me where …
   ☐ Do you know where … ?
4. ☐ Can you tell me how to find … ?
   ☐ Please tell me how to get to …
5. ☐ We're trying to find …
   ☐ We don't know where …
6. ☐ I'd like to know …
   ☐ Do you know where … ?

What are some famous places you've visited?

Real World Listening

PREPARE

Paula is talking about her visit to Turkey. Write the missing words.

money   way   inexpensive   communicate   scared

Now listen and check.

CD 1, Tracks 86–87

GET THE MAIN IDEAS

Order the sentences 1–10.

CD 1, Tracks 86–87

___ A Turkish man told her about a special restaurant.
___ Paula left the hotel by herself.
___ Paula was going to run away.
___ Paula followed the Turkish man.
___ They arrived at the restaurant.
___ Paula had a delicious Turkish meal.
___ Paula was feeling adventurous.
___ They went down a lot of little streets.
___ Paula couldn't decide which restaurant to go to.
___ Paula got scared.

RESPOND TO THE IDEAS

Paula says she decided not to be afraid to take chances when she's traveling in a new place. Do you think this is a good idea for a woman? Would you give a man the same advice? Why or why not?

WHERE IN THE WORLD?

1. The photos below are famous places around the world. Do you know what they're called and where they are?

2. Alone or in pairs, write or tell about one place. Imagine you went there. Tell your friend about the place you chose. How did you get there? What is nearby? What did you do there?

Warm Up

Write the word or phrase that describes each job.

great salary	danger	responsibility	teamwork
leadership	no commute	long hours	travel

1. I'm in international business. I go to other countries all the time, but somehow all the airports look the same. ___travel___
2. I'm a teacher. I feel that, in a way, the future of my students is in my hands. That's a heavy feeling. ______________
3. Being the boss is all about making decisions. The big office is nice, too, though. ______________
4. I'm a lawyer at a big firm. I work a lot, but it's worth it when payday comes around! ______________
5. I'm a nurse. I love helping people get better, but sometimes I don't get home until late at night. ______________
6. I'm a firefighter. All of us really count on each other during a fire. ______________
7. I'm a police officer. My wife worries about me, but I'm always careful. And I carry a gun. ______________
8. Working at home is great. I'm my own boss and I don't have to go anywhere to get to work. ______________

Now listen and check.
CD 2, Track 1

USEFUL EXPRESSIONS
When you're a ..., you get to ...
If you're a ..., you can ...
_______s make good money.
_______s don't have to ...
As a ..., you can learn a lot about ...

Think of a job. What are the benefits? Tell your partner.

Look at the pictures. What do you think each person's job is?

First Listening: Where did each speaker work?

CD 2, Tracks 2–6

Second Listening: Why was the job a good experience for the speaker? Check the main reason.

CD 2, Tracks 2–6

1. ☐ She had a flexible schedule.
   ☐ She could practice foreign languages.
2. ☐ He learned to use a cash register.
   ☐ He was part of a team.
3. ☐ He had a lot of fun on the job.
   ☐ He learned to work on computers.
4. ☐ She could ski a lot.
   ☐ She saw beautiful scenery.

What kind of job would you like to have? Why?

PREPARE

Sandy and Jennifer want to work for an online news agency. Look at their resumes. Who do you think is best for the job?

SANDY SPENCER
14 Everglades Drive
Atlanta, GA 30301
sweetsandy@yipee.tv
(555) 219-3363

Education
B.A., English Literature, University of Georgia

Work Experience
English Language Teacher, Zacatecas Language Institute, Zacatecas, Mexico
English Tutor, Georgia Learning Center, Atlanta, Georgia
Waitress, Sparky's Grill, Atlanta, Georgia

Sandy

Jennifer

JENNIFER LORANT
5625 Route 12 • Dekalb, GA 10146 • (555) 325-6713 • jlorant@netmail.net

EDUCATION
- B.A. Journalism/Video Production — Dekalb State University

EXPERIENCE
- News Producer, KPIQ — Dekalb, Georgia
- Education Reporter, WKRT — Cincinnati, Ohio
- Obituary Writer, Dekalb Morning Times — Dekalb, Georgia

Now listen and check. Who do you think will get the job?

CD 2, Tracks 7–9

GET THE MAIN IDEAS

Give a ranking to Sandy and Jennifer for the categories below.

CD 2, Tracks 7–9

(Use your own opinions.)

		bad	OK	good	excellent
Education	Sandy	☐	☐	☐	☐
	Jennifer	☐	☐	☐	☐
Experience	Sandy	☐	☐	☐	☐
	Jennifer	☐	☐	☐	☐
Personality	Sandy	☐	☐	☐	☐
	Jennifer	☐	☐	☐	☐
Desire	Sandy	☐	☐	☐	☐
	Jennifer	☐	☐	☐	☐
Connections	Sandy	☐	☐	☐	☐
	Jennifer	☐	☐	☐	☐

RESPOND TO THE IDEAS

How important is personality for getting a job? Experience? Connections? Luck?

WHAT'S MY JOB?

1. Choose one of the jobs below. Write the job on a piece of sticky notepaper and put it on another student's back. Someone will stick a job name on your back. (Don't look at it!)

2. Walk around the room. Ask questions about your job and try to guess what it is. When you think you know your job, ask, "Am I a ... ?"

Sample questions:

Do I work indoors or outdoors? What are the benefits (or advantages) of this job? Would you like to have this job? Do I make a high salary or a low salary?

When all your classmates have guessed their jobs, give a short summary of your job:

1. job name
2. where/how you work (inside/outside, with people/alone)
3. salary
4. advantages, features

Model

I'm an artist.
I work inside most of the time.
I make a low salary, but I like my job because I can be creative.

"It means a lot to me."

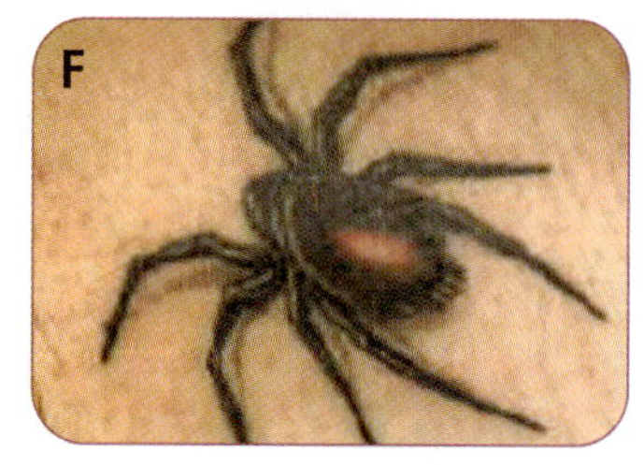

Warm Up

Match the pictures to the sentences.

1. L Hmm, that's kind of an interesting pin. It looks like a dog. It's a dog, right?
2. ___ I like this diamond ring. The one with three diamonds in it.
3. ___ This pendant has a Chinese character on it. I don't know what it means, though.
4. ___ That's a cool tattoo. What is it—some kind of spider?
5. ___ These earrings are porcelain and they're about 200 years old.
6. ___ The wooden bracelet is a kind of bluish-green color.
7. ___ This is a Navajo belt buckle. It's made of silver and turquoise.
8. ___ This is my favorite piece of jewelry. It's an Egyptian symbol that represents new energy.
9. ___ Hey, that's a cool pendant. It's got a lucky number on it. Lucky seven!
10. ___ Have you seen this lucky pendant I just got? It's shaped like a tree.
11. ___ What a lovely necklace. It looks like it's made of wooden beads.
12. ___ This pendant comes from Nepal. It has a lot of symbols engraved in it.

Now listen and check.

CD 2, Track 10

USEFUL EXPRESSIONS

It makes me think of ...
It reminds me of ...
I'm not really into ...
That's too ... for me.
I would never wear / get ...

Which things would you wear? Which would you not wear? Why?

Listening Task

Look at the pictures. What items do you see?

First Listening: Where does each item come from?

CD 2, Tracks 11–15

1

☐ Mexico ☐ Brazil ☐ Guatemala

2

☐ California ☐ Arizona ☐ Texas

3

☐ Korea ☐ China ☐ Thailand

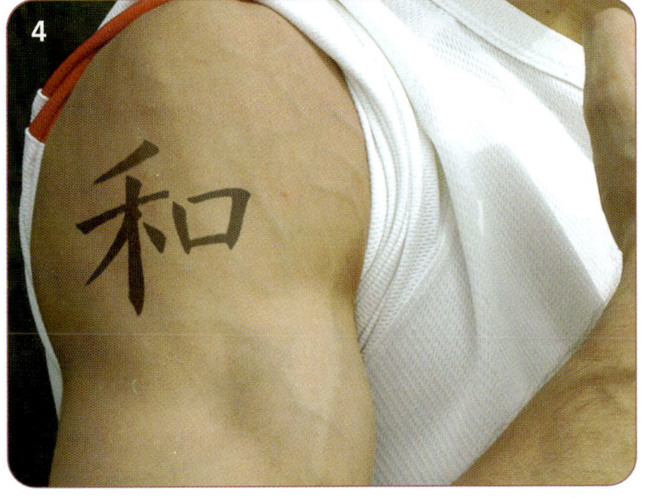

4

☐ China ☐ Malaysia ☐ Korea

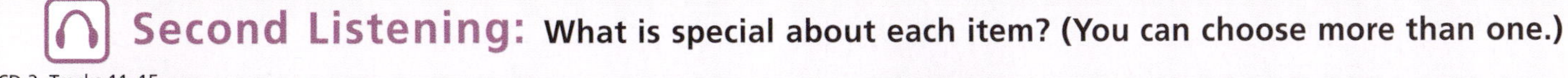

Second Listening: What is special about each item? (You can choose more than one.)

CD 2, Tracks 11–15

1. 

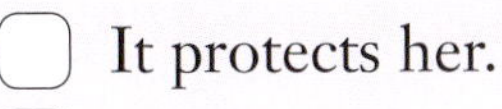

☐ It means "miracle."
☐ It protects her.
☐ She likes dogs.

2. 

☐ It's expensive.
☐ It is Navajo.
☐ It reminds him of a place.

3. 

☐ They are porcelain.
☐ They're flashy.
☐ They're from the Ming dynasty.

4. 

☐ It means "harmony."
☐ It represents his daughter.
☐ It's special ink.

What accessories do you have or wear? Why?

PREPARE

Look at the pictures. What do you think the bracelets stand for?

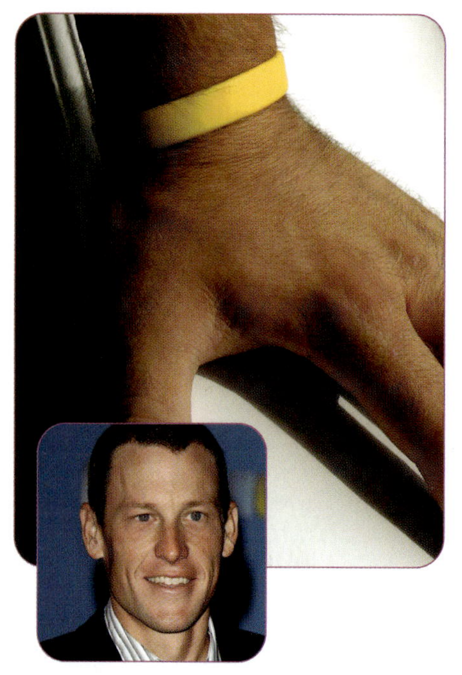

- ☐ knowledge is power
- ☐ attitude is everything
- ☐ help people with cancer
- ☐ support the Tour de France

- ☐ listen to rock music
- ☐ global unity
- ☐ fight to end poverty
- ☐ one person = one vote

- ☐ color of purpose
- ☐ practice = commitment
- ☐ commit to your goals
- ☐ collect antique rocks

Now listen and check.

CD 2, Tracks 16–19

GET THE MAIN IDEAS

Fill in the chart with details about each bracelet.

CD 2, Tracks 16–19

	Name	Purpose	Spokesperson
Yellow			
White			
Red			

RESPOND TO THE IDEAS

Do you wear a commitment bracelet? Do you wear anything else that reminds you of a commitment you've made?

IT'S SPECIAL BECAUSE ...

1. Do you have a special accessory, piece of jewelry, item of clothing, souvenir, or toy? Why do you have it? Fill in the chart.

2. Ask five classmates about special items that they have.

	What is it?	Where is it from?	How long have you had it?	What does it mean to you?
Me				
Classmate 1				
Classmate 2				
Classmate 3				
Classmate 4				
Classmate 5				

PART 1. Hearing the correct words.

Listen and write the missing words.

CD 2, Track 20

1. How much do I ______________________? I'm sorry. I'd ______________________ keep that to myself.

2. Excuse me? Oh, I'd rather not ______________________ my age.

3. I'm sorry, I don't give information like my ______________________ out.

4. My ______________________ is so cute. They say he looks a lot like me.

5. Their friends Bill and Angela ______________________ a 4-year-old boy last year.

6. Richard's ______________________ got married yesterday. His ______________________ is a doctor.

7. Last week they went to visit their ______________________ in Texas.

8. The bus stop? Um, you can walk there from here. It's just ______________________.

9. The post office? Just ______________________________ that first street.
It'll be ______________________________.

10. ______________________________ on Beach Road and go ______________
______________________. It's at 300 Beach.

11. Yes, being a doctor requires long hours of work, but I make a ______________________
______________.

12. He is the president of a big company. He has a big ______________________________
to his employees.

13. I love being a professional baseball player. It takes a lot of ______________________
______________ to win a game.

14. He wears a ______________________________ because it reminds him of his
daughter. She gave it to him for his birthday.

15. The picture of her children that she has on her desk has ______________________
______________ for her.

PART 2. Understanding conversations.

Listen to each conversation. Then circle the answers.

CD 2, Tracks 21–30

1. Why is Jenny's friend worried?
   (a) Because Jenny doesn't know Jose
   (b) Because Jose seems nice
   (c) Because Jenny came to the party to meet people

2. What do the speakers think about Chip?
   (a) They think he is cute.
   (b) They think he is creepy.
   (c) Both **a** and **b**

3. Who is Sarah talking about?
   (a) Her mother
   (b) Her brother
   (c) Her best friend

4. Which parent does Jane take after?
   (a) Her mother
   (b) Her father
   (c) Both her mother and her father

5. Does the British woman know where the place is?
   (a) No, because it's not in London.
   (b) No, because she's not from London.
   (c) Yes, it's next to Westminster Station.

6. Why was Paula scared?

(a) She didn't know where she was.

(b) People were staring at her.

(c) Both **a** and **b**

7. What did the speaker not like about the job?

(a) Talking to people

(b) Selling accessories

(c) It was tiring.

8. What kind of experience does Jenny have?

(a) Writing

(b) Video production

(c) Acting

9. What is the pin supposed to do?

(a) Protect you

(b) Perform miracles

(c) Protect dogs

10. Why did he get the tattoo?

(a) He likes Chinese characters.

(b) It represents his daughter.

(c) He wants to live in harmony.

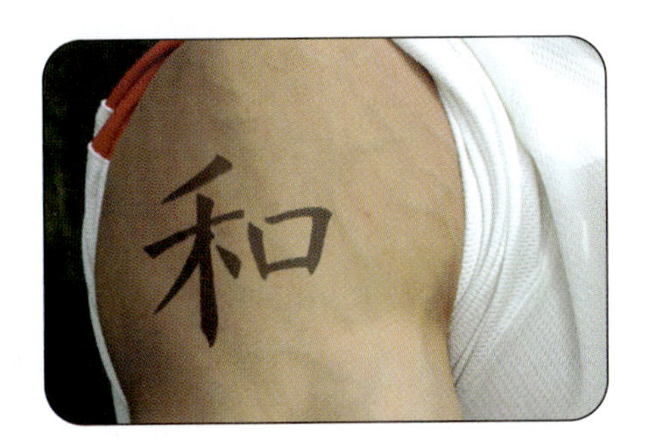

"They lost my luggage!"

Warm Up

Write the missing words and phrases.

baggage screening	carry-on	visa
airport security	economy	window seats
baggage claim	wrong line	
flight	metal detector	

1. Your attention, please. _______________ 275 to Miami will be delayed for two hours.
2. I'm sorry. There are no _______________ left. Would you like an aisle seat?
3. Oh, no, I think I left my _______________ bag on the plane.
4. I'm sorry. Your _______________ has expired. You can't leave the country.
5. Aagh! I waited for over an hour in the _______________!
6. You'll have to take this over to _______________ and have it scanned before boarding.
7. Excuse me. Can you help me? I can't find my luggage at the _______________.
8. I'm sorry. All of our _______________ seats are sold out. How about business class?
9. We'll have to get to the airport early. We don't want to get tied up in the _______________ and miss our flight.
10. Please put your carry-on bags on the belt and your shoes in the tray. Then walk through the _______________ while we scan your things.

Now listen and check.

CD 2, Track 31

USEFUL EXPRESSIONS

... was canceled.

I missed my ...

I'll never make it.

I lost my ...

I waited in line for ...

Work with a partner. Have you ever had problems when you were traveling? What happened?

Listening Task

Look at the pictures. What do you think is happening?

First Listening: What problem does each traveler have?

CD 2, Tracks 32–36

- [ ] He forgot his ticket.
- [ ] He forgot his passport.

- [ ] There's a long line.
- [ ] She's in the wrong line.

- [ ] The flight is canceled.
- [ ] The flight is sold out.

- [ ] His luggage is lost.
- [ ] His luggage is damaged.

Second Listening: What will happen next?

CD 2, Tracks 32–36

1. 

- [ ] He will call Susan.
- [ ] He will go back home.

2.

- [ ] She will miss her flight.
- [ ] She'll wait some more.

3. 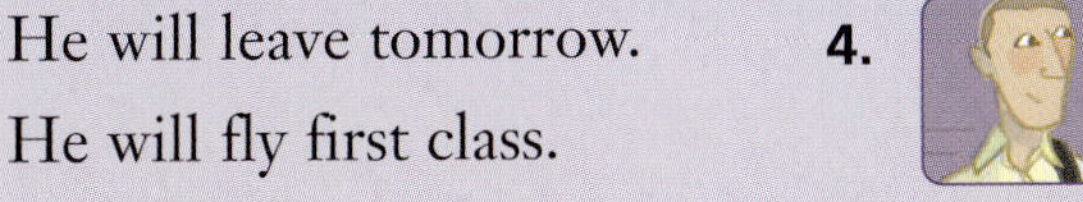

- [ ] He will leave tomorrow.
- [ ] He will fly first class.

4.

- [ ] He will have his luggage delivered.
- [ ] He will wait for his bags.

What are some other problems that travelers might have?

PREPARE

Look at the postcard. Trevor went to Costa Rica. What do you think happened? Write the missing words.

Dave,
You'll never believe how my trip has been! First, I ________ my passport! That was bad enough, but then I ________ my flight. After I finally took off, we had ________ trouble and had to ________ in Mexico City. I was stuck in Mexico City for almost a whole ________. When I finally got to Costa Rica, my ________ was missing. It seemed like a horrible trip, but then it all changed for the best.
Trevor

Now listen and check.

CD 2, Tracks 37–38

GET THE MAIN IDEAS

How was each problem solved?

CD 2, Tracks 37–38

1st problem: passport	2nd problem: flight	3rd problem: plane	4th problem: luggage
☐ His friend brought his passport.	☐ He took the next flight.	☐ They went on a different plane.	☐ He talked to an agent.
☐ He got a new passport.	☐ He went by bus.	☐ They repaired the plane.	☐ He bought new luggage.

RESPOND TO THE IDEAS

Do you think Trevor was sorry he took his trip? Why or why not?
Have you had a similar experience? What happened?

WHAT WOULD YOU DO?

1. Have you ever had something unexpected happen when you were on a trip? What did you do? Look at the situations below and write what you would do if they happened to you.

2. Ask a partner what he or she would do in the same situations.

What would you do if …	Me	My partner
… your car ran out of gas?		
… you forgot your passport?		
… you got on the wrong bus?		
… you fell in love with a local?		
… your wallet was stolen?		
… you missed your flight?		
… you couldn't find a hotel?		
… your luggage was missing?		

"What's for dinner?"

Warm Up

Some people are at a potluck dinner. Everyone has brought a different kind of food. What do they say about the things they eat? Write the missing words.

spicy	sour	creamy
crispy	chewy	raw
rich	salty	
bitter	plain	

1. Yum! This chocolate pudding is so rich and __________.
2. What a face! Is that lemonade too __________? Maybe it needs more sugar.
3. I'm surprised that they served the rice __________, with nothing on it.
4. You made this salsa? Mm. Nice and __________, the way I like it.
5. The cake was too __________. It had thick icing and a lot of butter in it.
6. Someone left the bag of chips open. Now they aren't __________ anymore.
7. Wait a second! Aren't you going to cook that first? You're not eating it __________, are you?
8. How are those cookies, __________ or crunchy?
9. Can I have a sample of this garlic ice cream? Yuck, it's __________!
10. I need a drink. The popcorn was really __________.

Now listen and check.

CD 2, Track 39

USEFUL EXPRESSIONS

It's easy to make.
I love making ...
... is my favorite food.
It's really ...
It's good for you.

What's your favorite party food? If you had to bring something to a potluck dinner, what would you bring? Why?

Listening Task

Look at the pictures. What kind of food do you see?

First Listening:

Who made the food?

CD 2, Tracks 40–44

1. ______________
2. ______________
3. ______________
4. ______________

Second Listening:

What does each speaker eat with the food?

CD 2, Tracks 40–44

1. ☐ salt ☐ salsa
2. ☐ soy sauce ☐ wasabi
3. ☐ hot sauce ☐ vinegar & soy sauce
4. ☐ beans ☐ vegetables

Ask your partner about their favorite memory of a food from childhood. When do they have this food now?

PREPARE

Maw-Maw is an authentic Cajun grandma who cooks the best jambalaya in the world. Look at the pictures. This is what goes into jambalaya. Do you think it will be spicy or sweet?

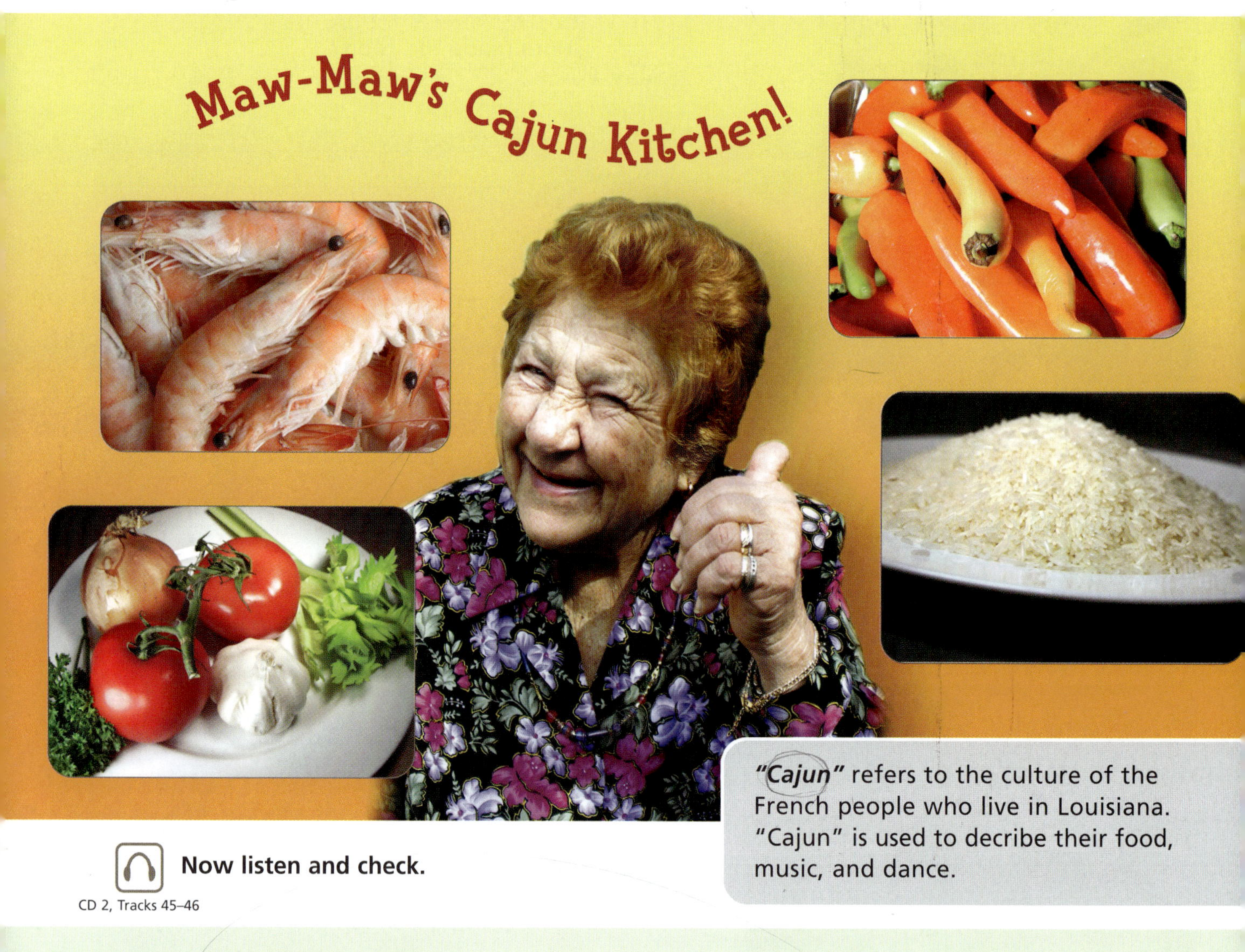

"Cajun" refers to the culture of the French people who live in Louisiana. "Cajun" is used to decribe their food, music, and dance.

Now listen and check.

CD 2, Tracks 45–46

GET THE MAIN IDEAS

Put the steps in order.

CD 2, Tracks 45–46

___ Bring to a boil.
___ Add tomatoes, sausage, rice, and broth.
___ Cover, reduce heat and cook on low heat for 30 minutes.
___ Cook until soft.
___ Serve with chopped green onion.
___ Brown meat or seafood in oil.
___ Add garlic, chopped onion, celery, and pepper.

RESPOND TO THE IDEAS

Jambalaya is a regional dish from the American South. Would you like this dish? Why or why not? What are some regional foods from your country that you like?

WHAT DO YOU EAT?

salmon	milkshake	apple	rice
hot sauce	popcorn	French fries	coffee
peanut butter	lemonade	cookies	potato chips
onions	butter	sushi	mustard
beef jerky	grapefruit	chocolate cake	carrots

1. **Write the foods under the words that describe them. Some words may go in more than one box.**

rich	creamy	sour	spicy	sweet
raw	**chewy**	**salty**	**bitter**	**crispy**

2. **Compare your answers with your partner's, or in a group. Discuss why you put the items in each box.**

3. **Choose a food, but don't tell your partner what it is. Take turns guessing what the item is by asking about how it tastes and feels.**

Example:

A: I'm thinking of a type of food.
B: Is it salty?
A: Yes, it is.
B: Is it crunchy, too?
A: Yes, it is.
B: Oh, I know. You're thinking of potato chips, right?
A: Yes, you got it.

UNIT 13 Schedules

Warm Up

 **Sheila and Tom are trying to schedule a meeting. Write the missing words.**

busy
booked
open
impossible
free
pencil
squeeze
light
full
tight

1. Hi, Tom, I can't make that meeting on Monday. My schedule is pretty __________. But Tuesday might not be __________.

2. Sheila. It's Tom. Tuesday, huh? Looks like I'll be too __________ then. I'm __________ solid all day. Can you make it Wednesday?

3. Hi, Tom. Sheila here. Uh, I might be able to __________ it in on Wednesday. It'll be __________, though.

4. It's Tom again. Something came up. Wednesday is no good for me. How's Thursday? Do you have any __________ time? Call me.

5. Hi, it's Sheila. I'm not sure about Thursday. But Friday's schedule is pretty __________. In fact, it's wide __________ after about ten in the morning. Let me know.

6. Hi, Sheila. It's me, Tom. Friday is good. Let's try for eleven. I'll __________ it in. Let me know if you can make it. Bye.

Now listen and check.
CD 2, Track 47

USEFUL EXPRESSIONS
When are you free?
Let's get together on ...
I'll pencil it in.
I can't make it.
I'm booked solid.

 **Make a plan to meet up with your partner on the weekend.**

Listening Task

Look at the schedules. Which schedules are full? Which are open? Where on the schedules are there free times?

First Listening: What event are they trying to schedule?

CD 2, Tracks 48–52

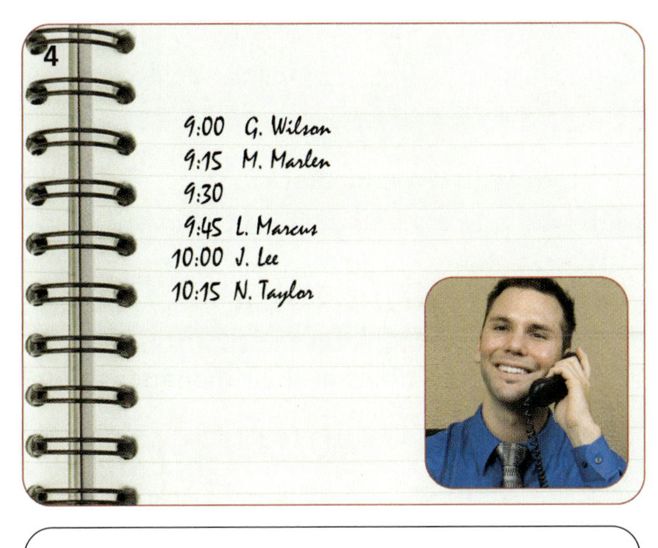

Second Listening: When do they schedule the event?

CD 2, Tracks 48–52

1.  

2.  

3. 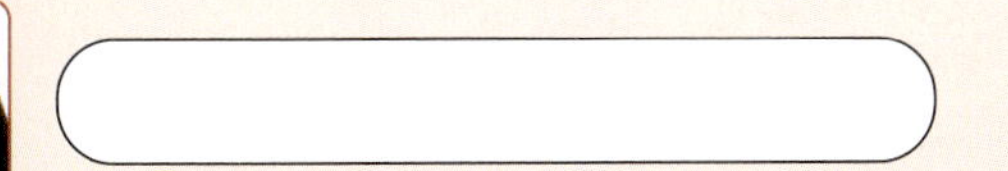

4. 

Which day of the week is busy for you? How about your partner? Who is busier?

PREPARE

Look at the picture. The rock group Pink is on tour in Asia. Write the cities they will visit.

Now listen and check.

CD 2, Tracks 53–54

GET THE MAIN IDEAS

When will Pink do the things below?
Write the times in their manager's notebook.

CD 2, Tracks 53–54

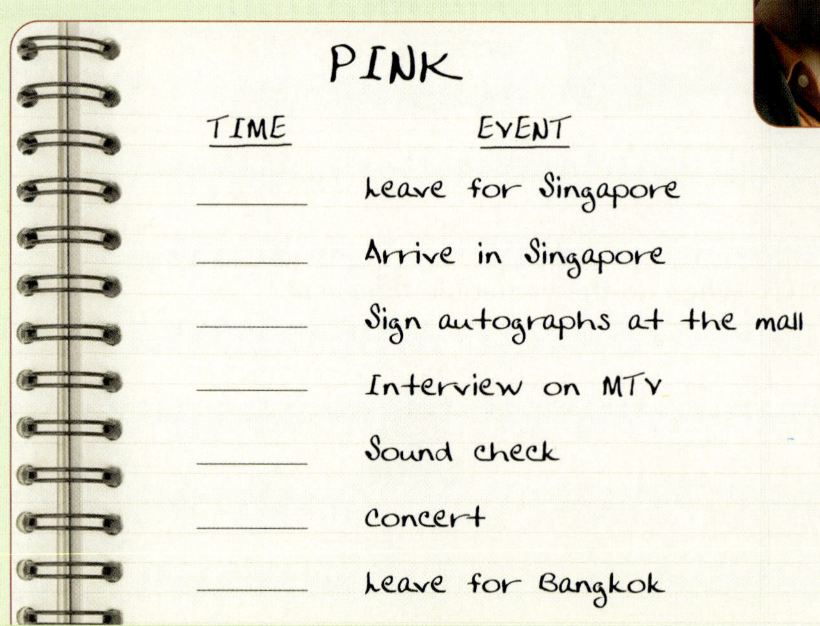

RESPOND TO THE IDEAS

Would you like to be a rock star and have a schedule like Pink's? Why or why not?

MY SCHEDULE

	Friday	Saturday	Sunday
Morning			
Afternoon			
Evening			

1. Choose three of the activities below and write them somewhere in your schedule above. Then walk around the class and ask your classmates if they can join you for those activities. Others will ask you to join them as well. You may only accept an invitation if you have an open space in your schedule. Continue until your schedule is full.

Activities

study	go to the movies	watch TV	have coffee
play tennis	go to lunch	have dinner	go to the beach
go hiking	go to a club	go to a party	play soccer
play computer games	go shopping	have a picnic	go to a museum

Model Conversation

A: Hi, Junko, I was wondering if you were free on Saturday afternoon?
B: I'm sorry. I'm booked in the afternoon. But I have the evening free.
A: Oh, I'm not open then. How about Sunday morning? Would you like to play tennis?
B: Sure!

2. When finished, tell a partner what your schedule is like for the weekend.

   A: I am booked solid this weekend. On Friday morning, I'm ...

UNIT 14 Weather

Warm Up

Look at the words. Which seasons do they usually describe? Write the words in the correct columns.

blizzard	muggy	humid	lightning	breezy
showers	chilly	flurries	damp	cool
scorching	thunder	freezing	overcast	rainy

Spring	Summer	Fall	Winter

Now listen and check.

CD 2, Track 55

USEFUL EXPRESSIONS

It's raining cats and dogs.
It's my favorite time of the year.
It looks like rain.
It's below freezing.
It's really nice out.

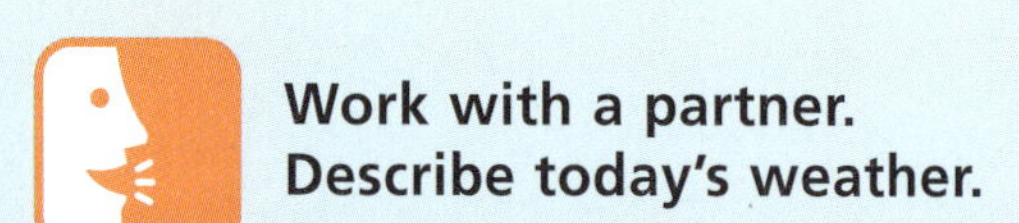

Work with a partner.
Describe today's weather.

Listening Task

Look at the pictures. Describe the weather in each picture. What season do you think it is?

First Listening: Write at least one word the reporter uses to describe the weather.

CD 2, Tracks 56–60

1

2

3

4

Second Listening: What activity does the reporter suggest?

CD 2, Tracks 56–60

1.  

2.  

3. 

4.  

What is the weather like on New Year's Day where you live? Do you like it?

PREPARE

Lena is looking at some photos of Alaska with her grandson, Alex. What do you think she will talk about?

☐ camping	☐ fishing	☐ blizzards	☐ skiing	☐ hiking
☐ bears	☐ swimming	☐ wolves	☐ snowmen	☐ puppies

Now listen and check.

CD 2, Tracks 61–62

GET THE MAIN IDEAS

What does she say about each season?

CD 2, Tracks 61–62

Winter	Spring	Summer	Fall

RESPOND TO THE IDEAS

Lena talks about childhood memories of different seasons. What special memories do you have of the seasons?

THE BEST TIME OF THE YEAR

1. What's your favorite season? What's your least favorite season? Why? Answer the questions below.

2. Ask a partner what he or she likes and dislikes about each season.

	Me	My partner
The thing I like the most about winter:		
The thing I like the least about winter:		
The thing I like the most about spring:		
The thing I like the least about spring:		
The thing I like the most about summer:		
The thing I like the least about summer:		
The thing I like the most about fall:		
The thing I like the least about fall:		

"It's so convenient."

Warm Up

Some people are talking about why they like where they live. Write the missing words.

conveniences
spaces
trails
suburbs
transportation
countryside
traffic
parking
trees

Mark

1. What do I like about living in the city? Oh, lots of things. First of all, there's lots of shops and movie theaters. And then you have public ____________ to get around, which is good, because there isn't much ____________ if you drive a car.

Bo

2. I don't mind working in the city, but I like living in the ____________. It's nice and quiet and there's more grass and ____________. You still get some of the ____________ of the city, like stores, coffee shops, and movie theaters, but not the noise or __________.

Raoul

3. What I like best about living in the ____________ is the wide-open ____________ and the fresh air. There's lots of green trees and hiking ____________. We don't have a shopping mall or a big supermarket, but there is a nice country store that sells organic fruits and vegetables, and fresh bread.

Now listen and check.

CD 2, Track 63

Where would you like to live? Why? Tell your partner.

USEFUL EXPRESSIONS

I like a place that has ...
I need to be near ...
I like a small-town feel.
I enjoy the pace of a big city.
.... is not for me!

Listening Task

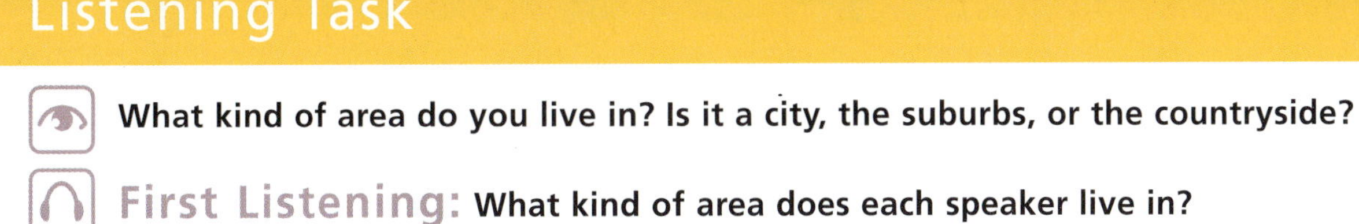

What kind of area do you live in? Is it a city, the suburbs, or the countryside?

First Listening: What kind of area does each speaker live in?

CD 2, Tracks 64–68

1

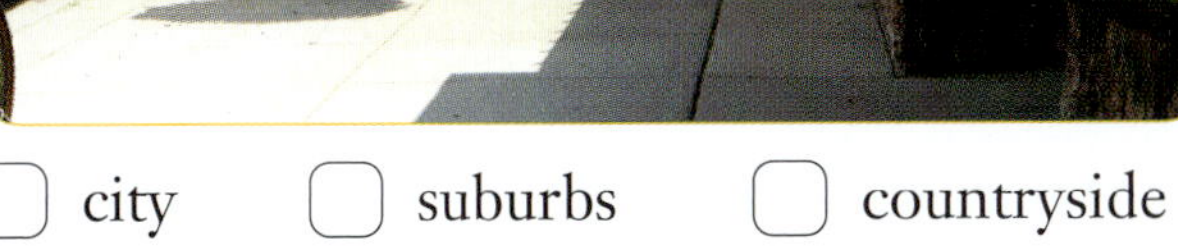

☐ city ☐ suburbs ☐ countryside

2

☐ city ☐ suburbs ☐ countryside

3

☐ city ☐ suburbs ☐ countryside

4

☐ city ☐ suburbs ☐ countryside

Second Listening: What is one thing the speaker appreciates?

CD 2, Tracks 64–68

1. 

2. 

3.  

4. 

What are some of the things you like about where you live?
Is there anything you don't like?

PREPARE

It is the year 2125. Julie and Fernando live on the international space station. They are being interviewed by a reporter. Look at the pictures. Which of the following do you think exist on the space station?

☐ mountains	☐ rainforests	☐ cities
☐ airports	☐ wide-open spaces	☐ shopping malls
☐ entertainment centers	☐ hiking trails	☐ cars

Now listen and check.

CD 2, Tracks 69–71

GET THE MAIN IDEAS

What do Julie and Fernando like about the space station? What do they miss?

CD 2, Tracks 69–71

Julie

1. What does Julie do for a living?

____

2. What does she like about the space station?

____

3. What kind of food do they have on the space station?

____

4. What does she miss about Earth?

____

Fernando

1. Where does Fernando work?

____

2. What is the weather like on the space station?

____

3. What kinds of things are in the rainforest?

____

4. What does he miss about Earth?

____

RESPOND TO THE IDEAS

Do you think people will be living in space by the year 2125? What will it be like? What will living on Earth be like?

PRIVATE ISLAND

1. With a partner or in a group, design your own private island. First write the details about your island in the chart, then draw your island.

Name:
Climate:
Landscape:
Animals:
Plants:
Population:
Transportation:
Entertainment:
Shopping:

2. Tell the class about your island.

PART 1. Hearing the correct words.

Listen and write the missing words.

CD 2, Track 72

1. Your attention, please. ________________________ to Miami will be delayed for two hours.

2. I'm sorry. There are no window seats left. Would you like an ________________ ________?

3. I'm sorry, all of our economy seats are sold out. How about ________________ ______?

4. Yum! This chocolate pudding is so ________________________.

5. You made this salsa? Mm. Nice and ________________________, just the way I like it.

6. I need a drink. The popcorn was ________________________.

7. Hi, Tom, I can't make that meeting on Monday. My schedule is ________________ ________. But Tuesday might not be impossible.

8. Sheila. It's Tom. Tuesday, huh? Looks like I'll be too busy then. I'm ______________ ____________ all day. Can you make it Wednesday?

9. Hi, Tom. Sheila here. Uh, I might be able to ______________________________
on Wednesday. It'll be tight, though.

10. In the spring, the city of Washington is ______________________________ and
there are frequent showers. The ground is very damp, so flowers begin sprouting.

11. When summer comes, there may be storms with thunder and lightning, or it can be
______________________________. Late summer gets humid, and people try
to avoid the muggy heat in the city by going to the countryside or the beach.

12. Winter brings freezing rain, low temperatures, and overcast skies. School children hope that
light ______________________________ will change into a blizzard so that school
will be canceled for a few days.

13. What do I like about living in the city? Oh, lots of things. First of all, there're a lot of shops
and movie theaters. And then you have public transportation to get around, which is good,
because there ______________________________ if you drive a car.

14. What I like best about living in the countryside is the ______________________________
__________ and the fresh air. There are lots of green trees and many hiking trails.

15. We don't have a shopping mall or a big supermarket, but there is a nice ______________
________________ that sells organic fruits and vegetables, and fresh bread.

PART 2. Understanding conversations.

Listen to each conversation. Then circle the answers.

CD 2, Tracks 73–82

1. Where are the speakers?
   (a) At the airport
   (b) In an airplane
   (c) At home

2. When does the man want to fly?
   (a) Tomorrow morning
   (b) That night
   (c) At 8 a.m.

3. The speaker is talking about ...
   (a) his favorite Chinese restaurant.
   (b) a dish his grandmother used to make.
   (c) how to make dough.

4. According to the speaker, in Mexico, the tortillas are ...
   (a) like cardboard.
   (b) always served with beans.
   (c) delicious when eaten by themselves.

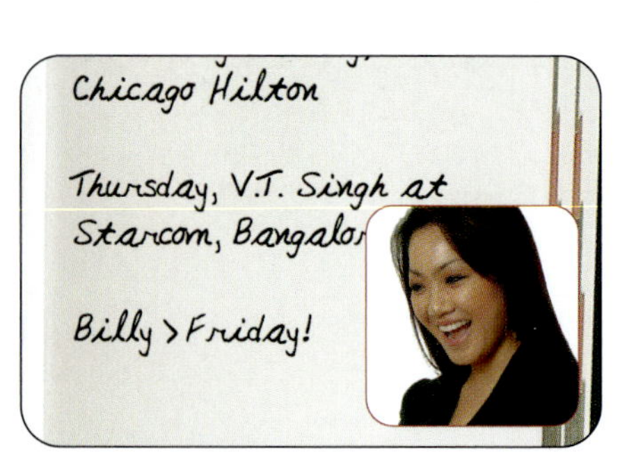

5. When will the speaker leave the conference in Chicago?
   (a) Tuesday
   (b) Today
   (c) Thursday

6. What day is Sheila free?
(a) Thursday
(b) Tuesday
(c) Friday

7. The weather in San Jose is ...
(a) unusually cool.
(b) rainy all day today.
(c) warm and damp.

8. Where is the speaker reporting from?
(a) Arctic, Canada
(b) Northern Minnesota
(c) Edmonton, Canada

9. Where does the speaker live?
(a) In a town named Jasper
(b) About 75 kilometers from Jasper
(c) Near the city

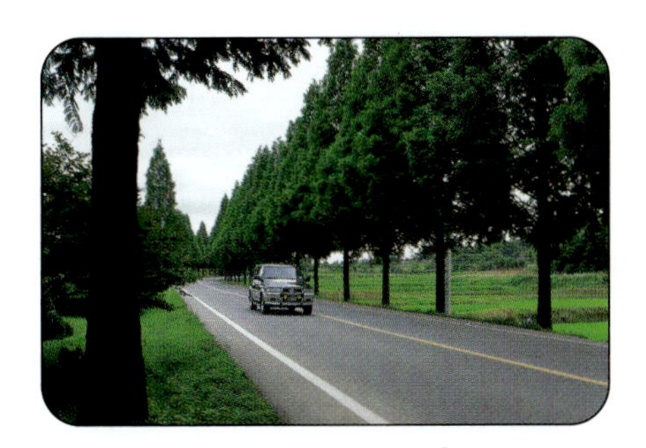

10. What does he like about living in the countryside?
(a) The shopping malls
(b) The fresh air
(c) The supermarket

Unit 1 Self-Study

Listen to the conversations. Write the missing words.

Self-Study CD Track 2

Part 1

Jean: Hi, uh, Robert?
Robert: Yeah? Oh, um, hi.
Jean: Sorry to __________ you.
Robert: No, no, no. It's fine.
Jean: You know, actually, I don't think we've __________.
Robert: Yeah we have. You're Jean, right?
Jean: I'm Jean. Wait, where?
Robert: You were in my Spanish class last semester.
Jean: Oh.
Robert: I sat in the back row, __________?
Jean: Yeah, that's right. You were the one that always came in late.
Robert: Uh, yeah. That's me.
Jean: Um, anyway, Robert, I'd like to __________ you to my friend Alicia.
Robert: Oh, hi.
Jean: Alicia's an exchange student from Mexico.
Robert: Cool. How long are you going to be here?
Alicia: How long? About a year. Until May.
Robert: Cool!
Alicia: Yeah?
Robert: I'm __________. Could you help me practice my Spanish?
Alicia: Uh, sure.
Robert: Really? Nice!
Alicia: If you're not busy tomorrow morning, we could practice here.
Robert: Perfecto!

Part 2

Alicia: Hi, Robert. How's it __________?
Robert: Hey, Alicia. Uh, thanks a lot for doing this.
Alicia: Doing what?
Robert: __________ me Spanish.
Alicia: Oh, yeah, right.
Robert: Yeah, I really love your ...
Alicia: Um?
Robert: Uh, your language.
Alicia: Oh! Oh, Spanish. You love Spanish?
Robert: Yeah, yeah. *Te amo*, uh, uh, *yo lo amo*? Is that right?
Alicia: Sure, close __________.
Robert: Cool. I've been practicing a lot.
Alicia: So, Robert, why do you __________ Spanish so much?
Robert: Well, um, there's this girl.
Alicia: Yeah?
Robert: And she was an exchange student here last year.
Alicia: Oh.
Robert: So, I'm going to __________ her in Spain this Christmas.
Alicia: Oh. great.

BONUS QUESTION

Alicia sees Jean after helping Robert with Spanish. What do they talk about? Write the conversation.

Unit 2 Self-Study

Listen to the quiz. Write the missing words.

Self-Study CD Track 4

Part 1

Here's a short personality quiz. This quiz will show some of your basic personality __________. Are you ready? Listen to each question, and then circle "a" or "b." Let's begin.

1. When you watch a movie, do you like to watch it with other people or __________?
2. Do you like to work on projects by __________ or with a group of other people?
3. When you go to a nice restaurant, do you make reservations first, or do you just go and hope you get a table?
4. When you get a new piece of electronics, like a camera or a computer, do you read the instructions before you connect it or just connect it without __________ at the instructions?
5. When you are working on a group project, do you offer ideas first or wait until other students give their __________?
6. When you have a question, do you ask it during the class or wait until another student asks the same question?

Part 2

OK, let's see how you answered.

Questions 1 and 2 are about __________. If you chose "a" on both of those questions, this shows that you are basically independent. If you chose "b" on both of the questions, this shows that you are dependent. You like to __________ on others.

Questions 3 and 4 are about organization or creativity. If you chose "a" to those questions, you are __________. If you chose "b," you're creative.

And 5 and 6 are about leadership. If you chose "a"s, you tend to be a __________, and if you chose "b"s, you tend to be a __________.

So what kind of person are you?

BONUS QUESTION

Are the results of the quiz accurate? Write a journal entry telling why you agree or don't agree with the quiz results.

Unit 3 Self-Study

Listen to the conversations. Write the missing words.

Self-Study CD Track 6

Part 1

Agent: All right, here's the apartment I told you about. As you can see, the building is clean and pretty quiet, so no one will bother you when you're studying. You'll have to get some __________, but not much.

Hye Jun: Hmm, I was really looking for a __________ place.

Agent: Well, sorry. This is all we have.

Hye Jun: Oh, it's OK. I could buy some furniture. The view's kind of nice, and it's big. And that's a subway station on the corner, right?

Agent: The B-Line. It's one stop from downtown.

Hye Jun: Oh, that's good. Um, how much is the __________ again?

Agent: Nine fifty a month.

Hye Jun: Hmm. That's kind of __________.

Agent: Well, that includes utilities.

Hye Jun: Oh, OK, well, I have to look at one more place, so I'll think about it?

Agent: Sure. Just call me when you decide. But this is a great __________, and I don't think it'll last long.

Part 2

Sara: So here's the __________. The last girl who lived here left her bed, so you can use that. And there's an old desk in the __________ you could have.

Hye Jun: Hmm, that would be good.

Sara: And this is the bathroom. There are three of us, so it gets __________ in the morning sometimes.

Hye Jun: OK.

Sara: And here's the __________. It's kind of messy today. Sorry. We had a great party last night. It was totally fun, but now we have to clean it up.

Hye Jun: Hmm. So what's the rent?

Sara: Three hundred a month, and we pay for water and __________, too. It's kind of like fifty a month each.

Hye Jun: That's not bad.

Sara: It's a pretty good place. And we have a lot of fun here.

Hye Jun: How long does it take to get to the university?

Sara: Oh, I ride my bike, so it's only about, um, ten minutes.

Hye Jun: OK, well, let me think about it.

BONUS QUESTION

What will happen next? Write the script for a conversation for the place where Hye Jun chooses to live.

Listen to the lecture. Write the missing words.

Self-Study CD Track 8

Part 1

Zack: Welcome to *Techworld*, the show that keeps you __________ on all the latest __________ in technology. I'm your host, Zack Newton. Our first guest today is electronics wizard Annabel Jenkins. Thanks for joining us today, Annabel.

Annabel: Thank you, Zack.

Zack: What new invention do you have to show us?

Annabel: It's called the MeBot.

Zack: And what does this MeBot do?

Annabel: The MeBot helps students. The MeBot can go to class, sit in your desk, take notes, and even __________ the teacher's questions.

Zack: Whoa, sounds great. And this MeBot kind of looks like you, too!

Annabel: Yes, I made this MeBot to __________ me, my body, my face. Some people even think it's me!

Zack: So, Annabel, what do teachers think of the MeBot?

Annabel: Oh, teachers love them. I think most teachers would love to have a class __________ of MeBots.

Zack: All right. Well, Annabel, are there any disadvantages to owning the MeBot?

Annabel: Hmm, right now the main disadvantage is the cost. This MeBot would cost about two million U.S. dollars. Not every student can afford that.

Zack: Yep, a little pricey. Well, thank you, Annabel, and good luck with the MeBot!

Part 2

Zack: Our next guest is Angela Park.

Angela: Hi, Zack.

Zack: Hi, Angela. Your invention is rather unique, I understand. It's called the BoyMeter. Is that right?

Angela: Yes, that's right.

Zack: And tell us what does this BoyMeter do, Angela?

Angela: It tells you what a guy is really __________. For example, if you ask a guy, "Do you like me?" and he answers, "Yes, I really like you," you can find out if he's telling the truth. Green light means he is telling the truth. Red light means he is telling a lie.

Zack: Whoa! Very cool! How does it work?

Angela: It's really easy. You place the __________ near the guy's mouth, and the __________ does the rest.

Zack: Fantastic! And it only works on boys, not girls?

Angela: No, it works on both boys and girls, but I call it the BoyMeter, because so far I've only used it with boys.

Zack: Ah, I see. Any disadvantages of the BoyMeter?

Angela: It's not __________ if the person has drunk too much coffee or alcohol. Those things just __________ the meter.

Zack: Oh, all right. Well, guys, be careful, and thank you, Angela. Well, that's our show for today. Join me, Zack Newton, next week on *Techworld*. Until then, good-bye.

BONUS QUESTION

If you could invent a robot, what would it be like? Write about it.

Listen to the conversations. Write the missing words.

Self-Study CD Track 10

Part 1

Wanda: You say you grew up in Africa?
Leath: Yeah, I'm from Lusaka, in __________ Zambia. My folks are from South Africa.
Wanda: Wow, what was it like there?
Leath: Oh, growing up in Zambia was "lacker." That means really __________ in Afrikaans.
Wanda: Afrikaans?
Leath: Afrikaans is the language, kind of like __________. A language that a lot of people in South Africa speak.
Wanda: Oh, Afrikaans. So, Zambia, is it cool?
Leath: It was so open, a really __________ place to be, lots of animals and sunshine.
Wanda: Wow! What animals could you see?
Leath: Just about an hour's drive out of town, you might see just about anything. At night you'd see leopards, and monkeys along the road, and sometimes you have to stop for elephants. There's quite a lot of rhino, and watch out for lions. They're very, very dangerous and they do take people from time to time.
Wanda: I'd be afraid to go there!
Leath: Yeah, but the people are my warmest __________.
Wanda: That's what everybody who's been there says about Zambia. "The people are so nice."
Leath: Oh, absolutely, yeah, in spite of all the __________ they faced.
Wanda: So do you want to go back?
Leath: Absolutely. If and when I go back, I'd like to travel around and see more of the country and its people. I'd take hundreds of pictures and maybe even put them in a book.

Part 2

Wanda: You were in Africa, too, weren't you?
Hannah: Yeah, I was in Zambia.
Wanda: What __________ you the most about being there?
Hannah: After I'd been there for two months, I felt like I'd gone to the moon, it was so __________. There wasn't much there. They didn't have cheese!
Wanda: Really?
Hannah: Yeah, and there were so many poor kids. You know, orphans whose parents had died of AIDS. It was so heartbreaking. And so they had to work.
Wanda: What kind of work?
Hannah: Oh, going out and picking up wood and selling it for cooking fuel. I really wanted to do something to help them.
Wanda: Yeah?
Hannah: Yeah, so I joined a group called Third World __________ Wives Group. I felt I had to do something. We started doing things, like raising money for the orphans. And we made __________ with people from other countries.
Wanda: Wow, sounds like you had a __________ experience. Would you ever go back?
Hannah: No, I don't think I could __________ it.

BONUS QUESTION

Imagine you are Hannah. Write a journal entry about how the group she joined helped the children.

Unit 6 Self-Study

Listen to the conversations. Write the missing words.

Self-Study CD Track 12

Part 1

Chip: Hey there.
Catherine: Hi.
Chip: Cool party, isn't it?
Catherine: Yeah, sure.
Chip: So, how's it going?
Catherine: Um, OK, I guess.
Chip: You know, you're really cute.
Catherine: Oh, um, thanks.
Chip: So, what's your _________?
Catherine: Catherine.
Chip: Catherine what?
Catherine: Just Catherine.
Chip: OK. I'm Chip.
Catherine: Hi.
Chip: So, Catherine, you _________ a good time?
Catherine: Yeah. I am. Great music. I love it.
Chip: Do you live around here?
Catherine: Yeah, sort of.
Chip: So where do you _________? In the city or in the ... ?
Catherine: Um, actually, I'd rather not say.
Chip: Well, listen, it's nice _________ you.
Catherine: Um, yeah.
Chip: So what's your phone number? You think I could _________ you sometime?
Catherine: No, sorry. I don't like to give out my phone number.
Chip: How about your e-mail address? Maybe I could _________ you an e-mail.
Catherine: Look, I don't want to be rude, but no, I don't think so.
Chip: Do you have a boyfriend, Catherine?
Catherine: Oh, there's my friend. I have to go.

Part 2

Catherine: Where were you?
Fiona: I was just getting a drink. What's the matter?
Catherine: Oh, nothing.
Fiona: I saw you talking to that _________ guy. Who was he?
Catherine: I don't know. He said his name was Chip. But he was kind of creepy.
Fiona: Really? How come?
Catherine: He was asking me a lot of _________ questions.
Fiona: Oh, so, is that bad?
Catherine: Yeah, he wanted to _________ my phone number and where I lived and all this other _________.
Fiona: Ooh, weird.
Catherine: Yeah. Oh, hey, I like this song. We should go dance.
Fiona: Let's go.

BONUS QUESTION

Rewrite the dialogue between Catherine and Chip with more appropriate questions.

Unit 7 Self-Study

Listen to the conversation. Write the missing words.

Self-Study CD Track 14

Nate: Are these your _________?
Jane: Yeah, that's my whole family.
Nate: Oh, you _________ a lot like your mom, especially your eyes. Very deep, beautiful eyes.
Jane: Oh, thank you.
Nate: And the same _________, same shape.
Jane: Uh, hey, I don't want to hear that. I may look like my mom, but I really _________ after my dad.
Nate: Really, in what way?
Jane: We're _________ very adventurous. My dad was, like, _________ motorcycles when he was younger, and he was in one of those, you know, motorcycle clubs.
Nate: Oh, you mean, like a motorcycle gang?
Jane: Yeah, but that was _________ he was married. I've been riding a motorcycle _________ since I was 17.
Nate: You? No way!
Jane: Yeah, I've _________ done stuff like that.
Nate: Oh really? Like what else?
Jane: Well, surfing, snowboarding. My dad and I even went skydiving once. We didn't tell my mom, though. She would have _________ us!

BONUS QUESTION

Jane tells her parents that she's going to go to the Amazon for the summer.
Write the conversation between Jane and her parents.

Unit 8 Self-Study

Listen to Paula. Write the missing words.

Self-Study CD Track 16

I was in Istanbul once—part of this __________ tour—and the tour guide told us to always stay with the group, not to go out on our own.

But one night I was feeling sort of __________, and I thought I'd try to find a restaurant and eat dinner __________ for a change. So I walked out of the hotel by myself.

I was looking around at all the restaurants and I couldn't __________ which one to go to. And this little Turkish man comes up to me and he says, "My nephew has a good restaurant. Come with me."

So I decided to __________ him. And we went down these little streets, and back, and it was getting dark, back __________, and I didn't know what was going on. People were starting to __________ at me. And I got really scared.

But I thought, "I'd just better leave." So I was going to run. And then __________, we rounded the corner and there we were at the restaurant. And it __________ up being the best Turkish food I had the whole time I traveled.

And ever since then, I haven't been so afraid to take __________.

BONUS QUESTION

Write a short description of a time when you got lost.

Unit 9 Self-Study

Listen to the conversations. Write the missing words.

Self-Study CD Track 18

Part 1

Mr. Chang: So, Ms. Spencer, your father called me and said you were looking for a job with us.
Sandy: Yes, well, I got back from two years in Mexico as an English teacher and I'm looking for something in __________.
Mr. Chang: I see. Why do you want to work for CNN?
Sandy: Well, it has a good __________, and I really like working with media technology.
Mr. Chang: Great. Tell me about your education. Which classes have you taken that have prepared you for this __________?
Sandy: Hmm. Seems like a long time ago. Well, I took a writing course at university, and um, a course on modern media, or something like that.
Mr. Chang: I see. Tell me about your __________ working with media technology.
Sandy: You mean, like, websites and blogs, and stuff like that?
Mr. Chang: All of the technology that's used in the __________.
Sandy: Well, I really like podcasts. I listen to them all the time, and I have a lot of favorite video websites that I visit every day. There's some very hot stuff out there.
Mr. Chang: OK, do you know anything about editing video, or preparing web broadcasts, or …
Sandy: Uh, well, I know how to watch it, and I'm sure I could learn how to make it.

Part 2

Mr. Chang: So, Ms. Lorant, why …
Jenny: You can call me Jenny.
Mr. Chang: OK, Jenny, why do you want to work for CNN?
Jenny: Well, first is reputation. I only want to work for a __________ with a sound reputation.
Mr. Chang: I see.
Jenny: CNN is the best, and I guess I just want to be part of that.
Mr. Chang: Great. Tell me about your education. Which classes have you taken that have prepared you for this position?
Jenny: Everything. Everything I've done has prepared me for this position. I have a double major in journalism and video __________.
Mr. Chang: Do you have __________ experience with media programming?
Jenny: Yes, a lot. I have a lot of experience with video production, editing __________, __________ video, web design. I produced news programs for my university's TV station and I've been a producer at KPIQ, my local station, for two years.
Mr. Chang: Hmm. Interesting.

BONUS QUESTION

Pretend that Mr. Chang is interviewing you for the job, too. Write the conversation.

Unit 10 Self-Study

Listen to the show. Write the missing words.

Self-Study CD Track 20

Part 1

Hello. I'm Parker Mills, and welcome to *Fashion Minute*. Today's topic is jewelry. The latest in jewelry fashion is the commitment bracelet.

I'm sure you've noticed the recent __________ on campus and around town. Everyone is wearing yellow. It's not an eye-popping fashion __________, but rather a simple, subtle, thin yellow bracelet with the words "LIVE STRONG" imprinted on the band. The idea for these yellow bracelets was originally conceived by Lance Armstrong, the seven-time Tour de France cyclist champion. As you may know, Lance Armstrong himself is a cancer survivor, and the founder of the Lance Armstrong Foundation. The LAF believes that __________ is power and __________ is everything. Their mission is to help people with cancer around the world get the practical information and tools they need to live strong.

Part 2

Recently, another commitment bracelet is making its __________, the simple white rubber bracelet with just a single word __________ on it: "one." This has become the symbol of global unity, a fight to end poverty and injustice. Supporters of the "one" movement include many __________ people, such as rock star Bono. They want people to __________ this bracelet to make a commitment: We commit ourselves—one person, one voice, one vote at a time—to make a better, safer world for all.

Part 3

Another kind of commitment bracelet is the personal commitment bracelet. Here's a commitment bracelet __________ by Kathleen Hall. According to Kathleen Hall, red is the color of __________. This bracelet is to be __________ as a visible reminder that you can accomplish any goal you commit to. Focusing on your goal takes practice and commitment. Fossil beads with a rich red carved antique coral focus bead and an __________ commitment box made to hold your goals.

Well, there's our "fashion minute." I'm Parker Mills. Thanks for joining us. And make your commitment today! Until next time, bye-bye.

BONUS QUESTION

Which of the three bracelets is most interesting to you? Write your opinion.

Listen to the conversation. Write the missing words.

Self-Study CD Track 22

Angela: I'm thinking about going to Costa Rica.
Trevor: Great! I went to Costa Rica once, but I had a terrible __________ getting there.
Angela: Oh yeah? Well what __________?
Trevor: Well, when I got to the airport, I realized I didn't have my passport.
Angela: Oh, no!
Trevor: So I called a friend, and he __________ into my house, got my passport, and brought it to me. But I missed that flight, so I had to stay __________ in San Francisco.
Angela: Oh, that's too bad.
Trevor: Yeah, so I got the flight the next day, and, of course, on the way, we had __________ trouble, so we had to stop in Mexico City, and I was __________ there for another, like, twenty-two hours while they got the part.
Angela: Gosh!
Trevor: And I mean stuck. They wouldn't even let us out of the airport.
Angela: You're kidding!
Trevor: I'm telling you. So, finally, I mean, like, after all this time, I get to Costa Rica two days late.
Angela: And don't tell me—your __________ isn't there.
Trevor: You guessed it. I go into the airline office to __________ and there was this really wonderful woman working at the __________.
Angela: Oh, yeah?
Trevor: And she was really nice and helped me out.
Angela: Mm hmm.
Trevor: And we sort of __________ it off.
Angela: Yeah? And then what?
Trevor: About two months later we got __________.

BONUS QUESTION

Retell Trevor's story. Add five new details.

Unit 12 Self-Study

Listen to Maw-Maw. Write the missing words.

Self-Study CD Track 24

Announcer: Maw-Maw is an authentic Cajun grandma from Louisiana who has won awards for the best jambalaya in the world. She'll share her secrets with you today, on the most popular daytime food show, *Maw-Maw's Cajun Kitchen!*

Maw-Maw: Welcome to *Maw-Maw's Cajun Kitchen!* Today we're going to make the most famous Louisiana Cajun __________, jambalaya! And if you're far away from your own grandma, you can learn how to cook this from me, your TV Cajun Maw-Maw.

First, you've got to decide how many people you're __________. The recipe I make will feed a big crew, say thirty people. If you don't have that many people comin' over, just cut it down to size. You start with a mess of __________ or seafood. We like pork in my house, but you can use crawfish, chicken, shrimp, or whatever you've got around. You __________ it all up in some __________ till it's nice and brown. Well, all right, the doctor says I gotta use olive oil, 'cause it's healthier.

Now two cloves of garlic, __________ up. Then you throw in some peppers. Make 'em hot peppers if you can get the __________ ones, and some celery, and onion. We put onion, celery, and pepper in everything here in Louisiana. And some andouille __________—that's nice'n' spicy, too—nice fresh tomatoes, some __________, and broth.

Now you let that boil, but just for a minute, then you cover the pot and turn the heat way down to low. You wanna let that __________ till the rice is soft, and dump some Tabasco on there. You folks from the North, that's our Louisiana hot sauce, made from red __________. We put it in nearly everything. So don't be afraid. If it's real Cajun cooking, your eyes should water when you take a bite. If they don't, it ain't __________ enough. Let's give it a taste test here. Whee-whoo! I guarantee that's spicy! Throw some cayenne pepper in there, too, while you're at it. All that pepper will keep you and your food healthy. So, you simmer it all for thirty minutes, then serve with green onion on the top and a bit more Tabasco sauce. Take a bite of this and you'll feel like you're back home in Louisiana!

BONUS QUESTION

You are planning a party for thirty people. What food will you make? Write the recipe for a dish and explain why you chose it.

Unit 13 Self-Study

Listen to the conversation. Write the missing words.

Self-Study CD Track 26

Tony: That was a great show! You were amazing tonight!
Sadie: I didn't know we had so many fans in Beijing. How many people were there, like 5,000?
Tony: No, more like 8,000!
Jess: Yeah, and they all wanted autographs. My hand is going to fall off if I have to sign another T-shirt.
Trixie: Yeah, me too. When do we get a break?
Tony: A break? This is show business. You don't get any breaks. And we need to be at the airport at __________ for our flight to Singapore. What time is it now?
Sadie: I think it's __________.
Tony: Well, get moving, then.
Sadie: But we need some sleep.
Trixie: Yeah! I'm so tired right now. I need to get some rest!
Tony: You can sleep on the plane. We'll get to Singapore at __________ in the morning. That's plenty of time.
Jess: That's only __________ hours, Tony.
Tony: Don't worry about it. You've got a few minutes before your next appearance. We're supposed to be at this big underground mall at __________.
Jess: More autographs?
Trixie: But we're going to be at a mall, right? Maybe we can do some shopping?
Tony: I don't think so. No __________ for shopping. After the autograph __________, you have an interview on *MTV Asia*. That's at __________, I think.
Sadie: Then what?
Tony: You've got to be at the stadium at __________ o'clock for a sound check. And you have to rehearse your new song, remember?
Jess: Oh, yeah, the new song.
Trixie: What time does the concert start, anyway?
Tony: Six o'clock.
Sadie: OK, so after the concert, we can rest, right?
Tony: Wrong. We have to catch a plane to Bangkok at __________.
Sadie, Jess, Trixie: Aaw!

BONUS QUESTION

Make a schedule for Pink that includes all of their events. OR write a newspaper story about Pink's tour. Include all of the events in the story.

Unit 14 Self-Study

Listen to the conversation. Write the missing words.

Self-Study CD Track 28

Alex: Grandma, what are these pictures?
Grandma: These are pictures of Alaska.
Alex: That's where you grew up, right?
Grandma: That's right, dear. I lived there until I was nineteen years old.
Alex: Is that you in this picture?
Grandma: Yes, that's me, and my sister, Ruth, and our dog, Kusko. That was out behind our house.
Alex: Wow. It _________ cold!
Grandma: Yes, that was in the winter, and it was cold. It _________ a lot! And boy, Kusko just loved the snow. Ruth and I and Kusko used to play in the snow for hours.
Alex: Did you make snowmen?
Grandma: Oh, we made some great snowmen.
Alex: Is that you in this picture, too?
Grandma: Yes, that's me and Ruth again. I guess we were both in high school then.
Alex: Where are you?
Grandma: We were hiking near Seward. We hiked a lot in those days.
Alex: But where's the snow?
Grandma: Well, it doesn't snow all the time in Alaska, you know. That was in the _________. Spring was a great time for hiking. It was a little _________, though.
Alex: Oh.
Grandma: Look, here's a picture of Ruth now, _________ her house.
Alex: That's Aunt Ruth's house? In Alaska? I thought everybody lived in igloos!
Grandma: Oh, no. Most people live in regular houses! Aren't those flowers lovely?
Alex: You mean, flowers grow there, too?
Grandma: Of course. In the _________ everything just blooms. It's sunny and the _________ is warm.
Alex: Warm? You mean, it was warm enough to go swimming?
Grandma: Oh, we all went swimming in July and August. The water was _________, but swimming was so much fun.
Alex: Was summer your favorite season?
Grandma: You know, I love all the seasons, but I think my favorite season was _________. The leaves in the mountains turning to gold–I always loved that sign of the _________ seasons. Look, here's a picture of the mountains near our house in the fall.
Alex: Wow, Grandma, I'd like to go to Alaska sometime.
Grandma: Well, Alex, I've got an idea. Let's go to Alaska together sometime.
Alex: Yeah, Grandma, that'd be great.

BONUS QUESTION

Write about your favorite season. Why do you like that season?

Listen to the conversations. Write the missing words.

Self-Study CD Track 30

Part 1

Sean: This is Sean McCain, live with Julie Morris and Fernando Martinez from Gemini One, the international space station. Let's start with Julie first. Can you hear me, Julie?

Julie: Yes, Sean, I can hear you.

Sean: Can you tell us what it's like __________ on the Gemini One?

Julie: The Gemini One is wonderful. It's not a lot different than living on Earth, really. We have entertainment, shopping, and lots of things to keep us __________ in Gemini City, where I live. All of the modern __________ that you have on Earth.

Sean: Can you give us some examples?

Julie: Examples? Sure, we have movie theaters, music clubs, restaurants.

Sean: How about food? Where does it come from?

Julie: I go shopping at the __________, just like people on Earth. You can get just about any kind of food here.

Sean: Is it expensive?

Julie: Well, the __________ stuff from Earth is–like watermelons. But most of the food is __________ or made here, so it's not too expensive.

Sean: And do you work up there?

Julie: I'm an astronomer, so the best thing about living here is being able to see the stars so clearly. That's important to me.

Sean: So is there anything you miss about Earth?

Julie: Yeah, I miss being able to see my parents for the holidays. It's expensive to fly home.

Sean: Thanks, Julie. Now let's see how Fernando likes living in space.

Part 2

Sean: Hello? Fernando?

Fernando: Sí, I'm here.

Sean: Now, Fernando, you don't live in Gemini City, do you?

Fernando: No, I live in the rainforest, just like I did back on Earth, in Venezuela.

Sean: The rainforest? Doesn't that __________ a lot of space?

Fernando: No, not at all. Without the rainforest we wouldn't be able to __________ enough oxygen for the people who live here on Gemini. I teach in the Rainforest Heritage Center, where kids learn about how important the forest is for human __________.

Sean: And does it actually rain?

Fernando: Uh, yeah, we have developed a weather __________ much like you have on Earth.

Sean: What other types of things can you find there?

Fernando: Well, there are __________ trails, waterfalls and rivers with all kinds of fish, and many of the animals that typically live in rainforests.

Sean: And do you miss anything from Earth?

Fernando: Of course. I really miss my jeep. We don't have gas-powered vehicles here. Only small electric cars and __________, but it keeps our air clean.

Sean: Well, we're just about out of time. Thank you for joining us today, Julie and Fernando.

Julie and Fernando: Our pleasure, Sean.

BONUS QUESTION

Imagine you live on a space station. Write a journal entry. Describe a typical day in your life.

Self-Study Pages Answer Key

Unit 1
bother, met, remember, introduce, wondering, going, teaching, enough, like, visit

Unit 2
tendencies, alone, yourself, looking, ideas, independence, depend, organized, leader, follower

Unit 3
furniture, furnished, rent, expensive, place, room, garage, crowded, kitchen, electricity

Unit 4
informed, advances, answer, resemble, full, thinking, device, meter, reliable, confuse

Unit 5
northern, cool, Dutch, healthy, memory, troubles, impressed, different, Diplomatic, connections, powerful, handle

Unit 6
name, having, live, meeting, call, write, cute, personal, know, stuff

Unit 7
parents, look, figure, take, both, into, before, myself, always, killed

Unit 8
group, adventurous, alone, decide, follow, alleys, stare, suddenly, ended, chances

Unit 9
journalism, reputation, position, experience, media, company, production, job, software, digital

Unit 10
trend, statement, knowledge, attitude, rounds, imprinted, famous, wear, designed, purpose, worn, attached

Unit 11
time, happened, broke, overnight, engine, stuck, luggage, complain, counter, hit, married

Unit 12
dish, feeding, meat, fry, fat, chopped, fresh, sausage, rice, cook, peppers, hot

Unit 13
twelve, eleven, four, four, nine, time, session, 1:15, 4, 10:30

Unit 14
looks, snowed, springtime, muddy, outside, summer, weather, cold, autumn, changing

Unit 15
living, busy, conveniences, supermarket, imported, grown, waste, produce, survival, system, hiking, trains

■ Coursebooks

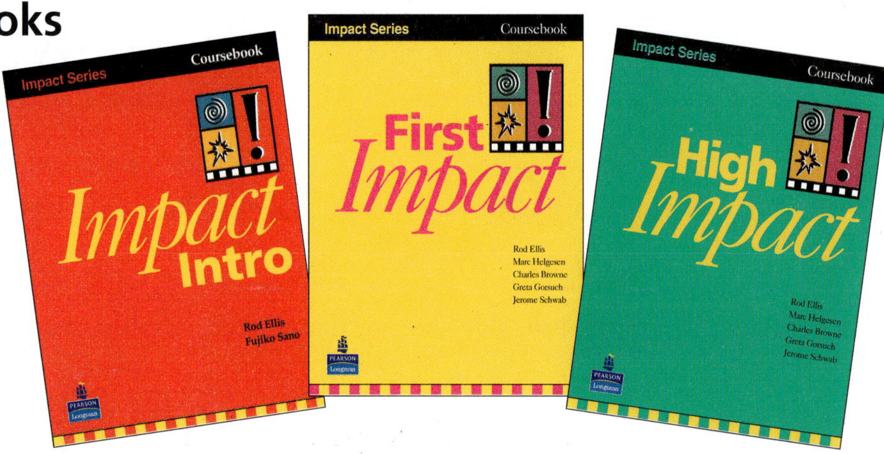

■ Skills Books

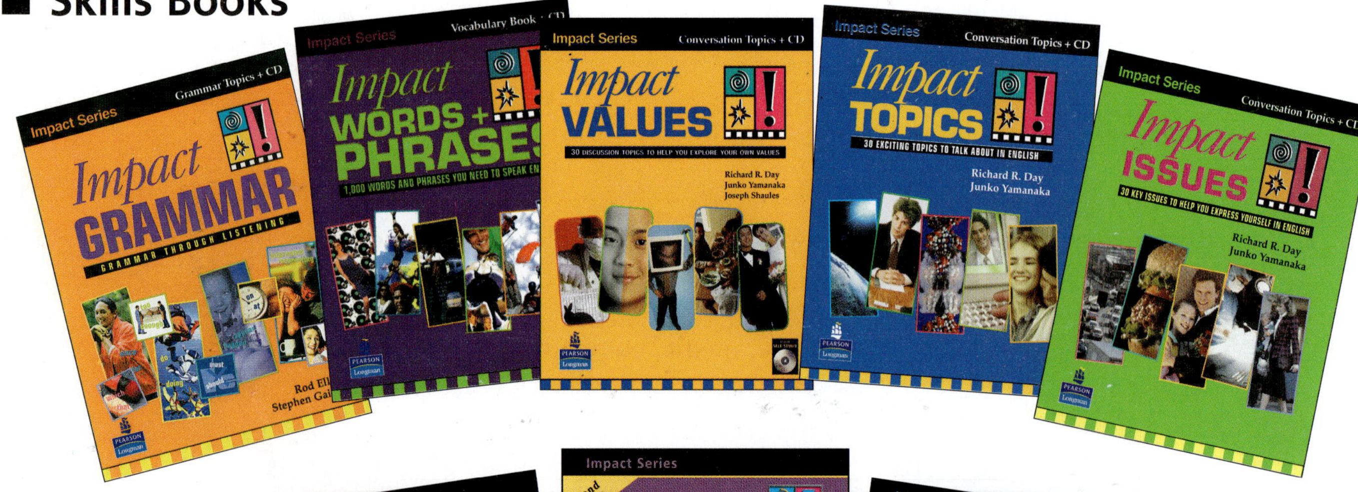

www.impactseries.com